Ethnologia Europaea

Journal of European Ethnology

Volume 24 1994

MUSEUM TUSCULANUM PRESS ❧ UNIVERSITY OF COPENHAGEN

Copyright © 1994 Ethnologia Europaea, Copenhagen
Printed in Denmark by AiO Print Ltd., Odense
ISBN 87-7289-305-2
ISSN 0425-4597

Editor: Bjarne Stoklund

Editorial Board   Carla Bianco (Italy), Jeremy Boissevain (Netherlands), Nils-Arvid Bringéus (Sweden), Joaquim Pais de Brito (Portugal), Wolfgang Brückner (Germany), Kiril V. Čistov (Russia), John W. Cole (USA), Esteva Fabregat (Spain), Alexander Fenton (Scotland), Béla Gunda (Hungary), Ueli Gyr (Switzerland), Tamás Hofer (Hungary), Lauri Honko (Finland), Orvar Löfgren (Sweden), Ján Podolák (Slovakia), Holger Rasmussen (Denmark), Klaus Roth (Germany), Lucienne A. Roubin (France), Bjarne Rogan (Norway), Martine Segalen (France), Zofia Sokolewicz, (Poland), Bjarne Stoklund (Denmark), Nils Storå (Finland), George B. Thompson (Northern Ireland), Ants Viires (Estonia), Günter Wiegelmann (Germany).

This journal is published with the support of Nordic Publication Committee for Humanist Periodicals.

Museum Tusculanum Press
University of Copenhagen
Njalsgade 92
DK-2300 Copenhagen S.

Editorial

Ethnization of Culture

The 5th SIEF Congress will be held in Vienna September 12th–16th 1994 under the title "Ethnologia Europaea" or "The Ethnic Paradigm and the Turn of the Centuries". In a circular published in Ethnologia Europaea 23:1 the President of SIEF, *Konrad Köstlin,* characterizes the theme of the congress with i.a. the following lines:

"At the end of the 19th century the ethnization of culture led to the institutionalization of the discipline. It was also a topic in the arts and crafts discussion regarding "national styles". At the end of the 20th century the ethnization of culture has taken on an unexpected importance, extending from regional and nationalistic movements and radicalism to the political use of "ethnic cleansing" ... This process of "ethnization" occurring around the turn of the century – the period around 1800 would have to be included here as well – is to constitute the central theme, illustrated by both "ethnographic" and "folkloristic" examples. Concretely, the question to be dealt with is the role of ethnization and our discipline (not only from a historical viewpoint) in the process of the nationalization of culture."

In the opening article in this issue of Ethnologia Europaea – which can be seen as a prelude to the conference – *Konrad Köstlin* develops the ideas and thoughts from the above quotation and discusses why ethnicity as a point of orientation seems to culminate at the turn of the centuries and in so-called crisis. He concludes that ethnicity promises a model which reduces complexity and offers a middle range identity concept: smaller than the world society but bigger than the isolated individuality of man.

The following five contributions are lectures given at a section on "Ethnization of Culture", organized by SIEF at the 5th International Conference on Ethnographic Nationality Research in Békéscsaba, Hungary, October 7th–9th 1993. In his article on "Politics, Culture and Social Symbolism" *Peter Niedermüller* takes up some of the problems dealt with by Konrad Köstlin. His point of departure is the role of ethnicity and nationality in Eastern Europe in the post-socialist era, and he ends his intensive analysis with the following manifestation:

"This analysis may be gloomy, but is free from illusions. However, being free from illusions it points to the responsibility of social sciences and of the ethnographers or anthropologists. We can not alter the world but live in the conviction that it is possible and worth speaking and writing about it, and that this mode of writing can be acceptable epistemologically as well as morally. That is, we can contribute to the creation of a morally more acceptable world by speaking about it adequately. This is not much, but not little either; this is the duty of all of us".

The other lectures from Békéscsaba all have a more limited scope. *Bjarne Stoklund* is interested in the role played by the great international exhibitions in the 19th century in establishing an "international grammar" of national culture and in selecting i.a. those "folk cultural" elements that came in general use as national symbols.

Gizela Welz changes the scene from the historical background to modern USA, where academically trained, so-called "public folklorists" are increasingly assuming a new role in cultural brokerage, mediating the relationship between immigrant cultures and the wider public. In her critical review of this recent phenomenon she raises the question, if these folklorists instead of reflecting the ethnic cultures "as in a mirror" are in fact inventing cultural otherness?

The two following articles are both dealing

with the use and the role of ethnicity in the daily life of people in Eastern Central Europe. *Žita Škovierová* has been studying ethnic consciousness and cohabitation in a Slovak-Hungarian village community, and *Balasz Balogh* has been doing fieldwork among Hungarian Germans from Transdanubia, who after World War II were by force resettled in Geretsried in Bayern. He is interested in the question to what degree their Hungarian German identity and way of life had been changed.

With the last two contributions to this issue we leave the field of "ethnization" to look at different aspects of popular world view or cosmology. Under the title "Mother help me get a good mark in history", *Jasna Čapo Žmegač* presents the results of an analysis of more than thousand invocations of Gods mother in the form of "grafitti" on the walls of a church in Osijek (Croatia). And *Ulrika Wolf-Knuts* outlines a popular cosmology on the threshold of the 20th century, based on a unique material that was collected in a Finnish fishing village in 1903.

The editor wants to draw attention to the fact that from volume 24 as well the editorial as the subscription address has been changed (see inside of the cover).

Das ethnographische Paradigma und die Jahrhundertwenden

Konrad Köstlin

> Köstlin, Konrad 1994: Das ethnographische Paradigma und die Jahrhundertwenden. – Ethnologia Europaea 24: 5–20.
>
> Obwohl die ethnischen Aspekte der Gegenwartskultur ihr Thema waren, sind die Ethnowissenschaften vom vehementen Aufbrechen ethnischer Argumentationsmuster in den politischen Bewegungen der letzten Jahre überrascht worden. Die Europäische Ethnologie hatte die ethnische Kultur als zwar wichtiges, aber doch eher freundliches Kolorit der modernen Gesellschaften interpretiert und dabei die dunklen Seiten ausgeblendet, die ein steigender Homogenitätsbedarf im Verlauf der Modernisierung und der sie begleitenden Differenzierung aktivierte. Ethnokulturelle Gefühle und die Renaissance der ethnischen und nationalen Solidaritäten bewegen die Menschen derzeit offenbar heftiger als gemeinsame Klassenlagen, ökologische Interessen oder Frauensolidarität.
>
> Die Jahrhundertwenden, in unserer Kultur immer als Wendemarken gedeutet und als Schwellen wahrgenommen, scheinen diesen Bedarf nach Sicherheiten zu aktivieren. Angesichts der Deutungen der Moderne als Individualisierung der Lebenswelten und andererseits als Uniformierung der Weltgesellschaft scheint das ethnographische Paradigma immer wieder seinen Reiz in der mittleren Reichweite zu entfalten, die Identität durch Differenz verspricht: als Möglichkeit einer zwar partikularen, aber doch kollektiven Identität. Der Artikel will schließlich nach der Zuständigkeit und Verantwortlichkeit der Ethnologie fragen.
>
> *Prof. Dr. Konrad Köstlin, Universität Tübingen, Ludwig-Uhland Institut für Empirische Kulturwissenschaft, Schloss, D-72070 Tübingen.*

I. Das ethnographische Paradigma

Mit dem Begriff "ethnographisches Paradigma" sollen die Instrumentalisierungen und die Nutzungen der Kategorie des Ethnischen in modernen Gesellschaften diskutiert werden. Die Etablierung der Kategorie "Ethnie" steht am Beginn der Moderne und ist bis in die Gegenwart als Kontrárstrategie gegen die Modernisierung genutzt worden. Sie begleitet den Prozeß der Modernisierung der europäischen Gesellschaften als basso ostinato, mal laut, mal weniger hörbar. Dabei sieht es so aus, als gewinne in Zeiten, die als "Krise" oder auch als "Wende" bezeichnet werden, die Ethnie als die scheinbar einfachste und ursprünglichste Kategorie an Orientierungskraft. Die Argumentation mit Ethnischem arbeitet mit der Plausibilitätsstruktur des Dauerhaften und Einfachen. Sie mutet in einer Welt der Veränderung stabil an und wird als verläßlich gedeutet und wahrgenommen.

An den Jahrhundertwenden akzelerieren offenbar die Krisengefühle. Denn diese Wenden werden in unserer modernen Zeitarithmetik als Skalierung der Epochen wahrgenommen. Überblickt man die letzten zwei Jahrhunderte, dann kann man beobachten, daß im Vorfeld der Säkulumswenden, zum Ende des 18., des 19. und dann am Ende des 20. Jahrhunderts verstärkt mit Ethnizität hantiert worden ist.

Man mag fragen, ob nahende Jahrhundertwenden den Wunsch nach Klarheit forcieren. Es läßt sich eine Art kollektiver kultureller Unruhe beobachten, die generell mit Zeitwenden verknüpft wird. Es könnten kollektive Ängste sein, die aus der Unordnung bei Übergängen in eine Ordnung drängen und das Chaos durch rites de passage zu regulieren suchen. Auch Individuen etwa räumen zwanghaft zum Ende des alten Jahres ihren Schreibtisch auf, arbeiten Briefschulden ab und beginnen an Silvester das neue Jahr mit guten, einfachen Vorsätzen. In unsere Kultur hat sich ein Summationsbedürfnis zu den Zeit-Wenden tief eingegraben: wir halten persönlich Rückschau und die Fernsehanstalten lassen das alte Jahr Revue passieren und fragen nach den Aussichten für das neue Jahr.

Gewiß trägt die Vermutung eines Zusammenhangs zwischen den Zeitwenden und dem Aufschäumen des Ethnischen nicht uneingeschränkt. Ethnische Klimakterien hat es in den vergangenen 200 Jahren auch zwischen den Wenden gegeben. Aber es sieht doch so aus, als ob sich das ethnographische Paradigma und die in ihm enthaltene Idee der ethnischen Homogenität für die Schaffung einer überschaubaren Ordnung und die Lösung von Problemen besonders anbiete. Am Ende des 20. Jahrhunderts entdeckt sich ein Europa aus lauter kleinen Ethnien, aus archaischen Stammesgesellschaften. Sie wollen dezentral in ihren Reservaten leben und hatten sich nur unter Zwang auf die Territorien der zentralisierten Hochkulturgesellschaften verirrt. Die Völker kultivieren, in Ost und West auf verschiedene Weise, ihre Unterschiede. Zwar spricht man in der politischen Rhetorik vom gemeinsamen Erbe ("mitteleuropeo"), doch weigert man sich, Gemeinsamkeit zu praktizieren. Regionale Speisen haben Hochkonjunktur, regionale Sprachen und Dialekte werden gepflegt und Minderheiten werden in Kulturotopen unter gesetzlichen Schutz gestellt. Überall gießt man die eigenen Wurzeln, pflegt eine "eigen" genannte Geschichte. Regionale Trachten geben Anregung für die Mode. Kleidung, Essen, Wohnen: alle Arten von demonstrativem Konsum zitieren Ethnisches, spielen mit ethnischen Akzenten und scheinen so entscheidend für die symbolische Praxis moderner Identität zu sein.

Die offenbar gewordene Tendenz zur Pluralisierung der Lebenswelten hat in den modernen Gesellschaften zur Suche nach stabilen Gemeinsamkeiten geführt. Bereits in den regionalistischen Bewegungen der 1970er Jahre mit ihren Forderungen nach Dezentralität, Territorialität, regionaler Autonomie und Kleinräumigkeit ("small is beautiful") konnte man einen aufgefrischten ethnischen Akzent entdecken, der mehr Aufmerksamkeit verdient hätte. Er operierte mit der heimatlichen Verwurzelung der Menschen ("Heimat und Identität") und leitete davon unter der Hand Vorrechte der Eingesessenen ab. Die Pflege des Regionalen, als freundliches Spiel betrieben, verleiht auch der Inhumanität, die uns derzeit unter dem Signum des Ethnischen begegnet, Legitimität.

Offenbar war es eine folkloristisch getönte, ethnozentrische Blindheit, der viele von uns aufgesessen waren. Das Attribut "ethnisch" wurde vielfach auch in Forschungsstrategien zur Kategorie für regionale und soziale Abgrenzungen und Besonderheiten etwa im Sinne von "regionalkulturell" benutzt. Ethnische Merkmale und ihre Ausdrucksformen, die man Volkskultur nannte, galten als freundliches Dekor, als eine Kraft, die aus der Vergangenheit in die moderne Gegenwart reichte und dort eine willkommene Farbigkeit bewirkte. Der Slogan "Folklore verbindet die Völker" meinte vor allem eine Ebene des Verstehens, auf der – bei allen Unterschieden im Detail – ein Akzent auf den Gemeinsamkeiten zwischen den Völkern liegen sollte. In der Folklore hatten die Völker ihre Sonntagsseiten vorgeführt – sich selbst und den anderen. Folklore war das Gute, Freundliche, Menschliche, das sich die Gesellschaften zur Erklärung ihrer selbst aus den jeweiligen Traditionen ausgewählt hatten. Nationalistische Auseinandersetzungen oder gar "ethnische Säuberungen" schienen in diesem Konzept keinen Platz zu haben.

Bei der Suche nach Gemeinsamen scheint die Wiedergewinnung der Gemeinschaft im Vordergrund zu stehen, wie sie sich auch in der Philosophie des amerikanischen Kommunitarismus zeigt. Das Angebot der ethnischen Gemeinsamkeit ist ein Konzept vom Ende des 18. Jahrhunderts, das zur Bildung von Nationalstaaten und als erster Schritt in die Moderne hilfreich gewesen war. Die Ethnie mit ihrer Idee der Einheitskultur mag Krisen zu Beginn der Modernisierung aufgefangen haben. Heute aber wird in der ethnisch motivierten Absage an das Konzept der Moderne eine geschlossene Gesellschaft imaginiert, die, fundamentalistisch auf Religion und Ethnie gegründet, das Leben des Individuums ordnen soll. Ob eine kaum modifizierte Neuauflage eines 200 Jahre alten ethnischen Gedankens die Krise unserer Zeit lösen und mehr als nur eine höchst fragwürdige Homogenisierung bieten kann, muß zweifelhaft bleiben.

Man hatte sich also getäuscht, wir hatten uns geirrt: unter der Decke der freundlich-harmlosen Folklore schlummerte offenbar etwas, was man "kollektive Erinnerung" nannte; eine Potenz, die offenbar leicht abrufbar und vor allem stärker war, als man angenommen hatte und die zerstörerisch wirkte. Schon vor einigen Jahren zeigte sich, daß die von dem Musikwissenschaftler Landsbergis aktivierte Folklore Litauens nicht nur ihren Beitrag zur Befreiung des Landes geleistet hatte, sondern auch die Vertreibung der Fremden zum Ziele hatte. Solche Nutzung der Folklore mußte hellhörig machen. Das ehemalige Jugoslawien macht den Eindruck, als sei es ein Hort der Traditionen; "ethnische Säuberungen" werden (nicht nur dort) oft kriegerisch vollzogen und mit ethnischer Kultur, mit Folklore begründet. Die Sprache der alten Heldenlieder legitimiert heutige Gewalt. Die Folkloristen des 19. Jahrhunderts hatten Heldenlieder als nationale Gesänge gesammelt. Heute werden die Verstümmelungen von Menschen nach diesen Texten praktiziert und durch den Verweis auf die ethnische Folklore mythisch unterlegt und damit gerechtfertigt.

Dabei geht es am Ende des 20. Jahrhunderts nicht nur um die Ängste der kleinen Völker und den kulturellen Schutz von Minderheiten. Auch die großen Ethnien signalisieren Bedrohtheit; Angst scheint sich in ihnen breitzumachen. Rechtsradikalismus und überwunden geglaubte Allianzen tun sich auf. Regressionen in alte Muster, die Vergangenheit für Zukunft ausgeben, lassen sich vielerorts beobachten. Folklore, die man als harmloses und freundliches Spiel verstanden hatte, wird zur Waffe. Vom "Dialekt als Waffe" hatte der elsässische Poet und Regionalist André Weckmann vor 20 Jahren gesprochen, ohne daß man ihn damals recht ernst genommen hätte.

Das ethnographische Paradigma hat also eine zusätzliche und ungeahnte Brisanz bekommen, seit ethnisch argumentiert wird. Eine Welle von Flüchtlingen, die Armut und ethnische Kriege ("Bürgerkriege") aus ihrer Heimat treiben, kommt auf die westlichen Industrienationen zu. Sie löst dort wiederum ethnische Argumentationsmuster aus, die in der Asylfrage kulminieren. Sprachbilder wie die Rede von der "Welle von Flüchtlingen" und von der "Asylantenflut" spielen mit Ängsten. Die Formeln unterstellen, es handele sich dabei um Naturgewalten, denen man machtlos ausgeliefert sei. Soziale Konflikte, und um solche handelt es sich zwischen Metropolen und Peripherien, werden als ethnische Konflikte traktiert. Die fremde, "andere" Kultur wird ethnisiert. Ethnisch genannte Konflikte, Verteilungskämpfe zwischen arm und reich, sind überall in Europa, ob in Italien, Frankreich, Deutschland, Irland, Spanien, Schweden oder anderswo auf der Tagesordnung.

Längst noch nicht ist entschieden, ob und in welchem Maße europäische Politik einem demokratischen Kurs folgen kann. Längst ist noch nicht entschieden, ob demokratische Aufbrüche in Osteuropa in populistisch-völkische Nationalismen fallen werden. Denkbar ist jedoch, daß die Argumentation mit dem ethnographischen Paradigma die westlichen Demokratien brüchig werden läßt. Angehörige der intellektuellen Eliten, Philosophen und Historiker, haben dies höchst subtil seit einigen Jahren vorbereitet. Nationalismen dienen als Puffer gegen die europäische Einigung. Immer häufiger wurde in den letzten Jahren der Nationalismus als die einzige wirkliche antikommunistische Bewegung in Europa gerühmt. Der deutsche Historiker Ernst Nolte hatte vor einigen Jahren den Nationalsozialismus als die bislang einzige entscheidende antikommunistische Kraft in Europa bezeichnet und damit in der Bundesrepublik eine hitzige Kontroverse, den sogenannten "Historikerstreit", ausgelöst. Nolte hat kürzlich nachgesetzt: nicht nur der liberal-emanzipatorische Nationalismus des frühen 19. Jahrhunderts sei historisch legitim, sondern auch der völkische Nationalismus habe sein "historisches Recht".

Aber auch anthropologische Konstanten

werden entdeckt. Überall, so heißt es, hätten sich die Angehörigen des eigenen Stammes als "Menschen" bezeichnet, hört man kulturanthropologisch argumentieren und raunen. Die anderen, das waren die Nicht-Menschen, daraus wird geschlossen, daß Fremdenfeindlichkeit eine ganz natürliche Sache sei. Das Argumentieren mit Ethnizität verschärft sich zudem, seit vermehrt (wie auch in der Frauenforschung) biologisch-naturwissenschaftlich argumentiert wird. Aggression und Territorialität werden wie Naturtriebe gerechtfertigt. Eine breite Welle biologistischer Argumentation kommt auf uns zu, die alle Aggressivität als naturhaft versteht und, weil sie unausweichlich sei, entschuldigt: die Menschen seien so angelegt. Es scheint kein Entrinnen mehr zu geben. Das Ethnische, biologistisch gestützt, scheint zum Schicksal zu werden.

Je komplexer, je unübersichtlicher und angstmachender das Individuum und die Gesellschaften die Wirklichkeit erleben, umso eindeutiger und einfacher müssen die Interpretationsangebote sein. Angst verspüren die Menschen (auch das ist Deutung) offenbar verstärkt an den säkularen Nachdenk-Wenden. Das Ethnische als einfaches Angebot besticht durch seine Plausibilitätsstruktur: alle verstehen es, weil es die Menschen in gute und böse einteilt. Biologische und geographische Merkmale, das ius sanguinis und das ius soli werden diskutiert, Blut und Boden sind gefragt.

So sind Volk und Volkskultur, Ethnie, Region und Nation wieder zu Kategorien geworden, die in der politischen Sprache Resonanz finden. Das kann uns nicht unberührt lassen. Wir sollten uns fragen, warum sich dazu bisher nur Politikwissenschaft und Soziologie, aber kaum die Volkskunde, die Europäische Ethnologie geäußert hat; so als hätte dies alles mit unserem Fach und den von ihm angezettelten Diskursen überhaupt nichts zu tun. Bleibt es für uns wieder bei den Harmlosigkeiten? Wie sieht es aus, wenn es ernst wird? Was hat die Volkskunde zu sagen, wenn das Ethnische blutig wird? Oder fällt das Böse nicht mehr in das Ressort der Europäischen Ethnologie? Zieht sie sich in den Alltag der Mikrostudien zurück? Reicht sie wieder nicht über Pflug und Hacke, Hausbau, Wohnen und Nahrung, Volkserzählung, Keramik, Lied und Tracht und ihre modernen Äquivalente hinaus? Übersieht die Volkskunde etwa, daß nicht einmal dieser Kanon harmlos ist? Häufig genug hat man in Vergangenheit und Gegenwart mit volkskundlicher Atlasforschung und den Belegkarten für die Verbreitung kultureller Elemente territoriale Ansprüche untermauert. Hausformen und ihre Verbreitung wurden zum Beleg für ethnische Siedlungsgebiete und, daraus abgeleitet, zu territorialen Ansprüchen; Verbreitungskarten von Trachten- und Wirtschaftsformen, von Formen und Geräten zur Bodenbearbeitung dienten als Vorspiel für den Versuch, neue Grenzen zu ziehen, "Kulturräume" zu erobern.

Es kann kein Zufall sein, daß am Beginn der bürgerlichen Moderne, also gegen Ende des 18. Jahrhunderts, dann noch einmal am Ende des 19. und nun, überraschend, am Ende des 20. Jahrhunderts das ethnographische Paradigma in einer Reihe von Ländern so bedeutungsvoll wird. Die gegenwärtige Nutzung des ethnographischen Paradigmas sollte uns auf den Plan rufen. Das Ethnographische ist ja nicht nur Zitat oder Zutat. Wir erleben heute ein auf das fin de siècle gestimmtes Europa, in dem die demokratischen Aufbrüche und Umbrüche unerwartet nicht nur nationale und nationalistische, sondern vor allem ethnische Kategorien erneuert haben. Sie argumentieren mit Sprache, Folklore, Blut und Boden und lassen "Fremdes" nicht gelten.

Auch die Staaten Westeuropas zeigen Bewegungen, die man als nativistisch bezeichnen könnte. Sie erweisen sich damit als moderne Industrienationen mit unbewältigtem Fortschritt. Mit nur wenig anderer Begründung als in Osteuropa erleben auch dort ethnische Merkmale eine auffällige Renaissance. Die Gesetze zur Rettung des französischen Baguettes, die Versuche, nationale gegen fremde (Mc Donalds!) Speiseangebote durchzusetzen, der Schutz der einheimischen Popsongs wie die Fremdenfeindlichkeit des "Ausländer raus!" tun so, als hätte man nur den eigenen Garten sauber zu halten. Sie lassen erkennen, wie desorientiert solche Strategien auf die Herausforderungen der Modernisierung reagieren. Es gilt daher, die symbolischen Sichtweisen aufzusuchen, die von den intellektuellen Agenturen entworfen wurden, um "Identität" und Zugehörigkeit zuzuteilen und zu verweigern. Zu diesen Agenturen gehört auch die Volkskunde.

Die politische, unsere alltägliche und auch die wissenschaftliche Orientierungslosigkeit sind beeindruckend und erschreckend. Das Ethnische, das die Rückkehr als Fortschritt anpreist, verlangt eine kritische Analyse. Was aber haben die Ethnowissenschaften dazu beigetragen, wo sind sie verantwortlich? Was haben sie an Erklärungen, Theorien, Begriffen, Methoden und Modellen anzubieten? Die neu aufbrechenden, latent vorhandenen, unterdrückten und die inszenierten Traditionslinien haben neue Wahrnehmungsweisen entstehen lassen, bringen neue Sozialstrukturen hervor. Ethnische Parameter übersteigen nationalstaatliche Grenzen. Religiös-ethnische Merkmale wirken auf neue Weise desintegrierend und integrierend, lassen staatliche Zusammenhänge zerfallen und bilden neue. Traditionen (heilig und deshalb erstarrt) dienen zur Rechtfertigung der Regression (die etwa Frauen in traditionelle Rollen zurückverweist). Neue und alte Mythen und Symbole, auch hier ein Aufschwung, und eine gewaltige Geschichtenkultur des Eigenen sollen Legimität herstellen.

Die erstaunliche und anhaltende Energie, mit der in unseren Tagen unter dem Etikett der "ethnischen Säuberung" soziale Konflikte und Verteilungskämpfe als ethnische Auseinandersetzungen interpretiert und damit kulturell begründet werden, rechtfertigen und verlangen, der Entstehungsgeschichte dieser Energie, die in der Ethnizität zu stecken scheint, nachzugehen. Dabei soll nicht nur nach einem historischen Ort dieser Kraft gefragt werden, die solche Potenzen in Kollektiven entstehen läßt. Eine Bemerkung, die Georg Simmel, ein Soziologe der Jahrhundertwende, einmal gemacht hatte, setze ich als Prämisse an. Die Menschen, so Simmel, schöpften Kräfte aus Einrichtungen, die sie zuvor mit diesen Kräften ausgestattet hätten. Die Ethnie also kann als Kraftpotential erst wirksam werden, nachdem sie als Idee stark gemacht worden ist. Ich will damit nicht behaupten, daß die Ethnie nur in den Köpfen der Menschen existiere, aber wir wissen, daß die Wirkung von Begriffen etwas mit der Macht der Deutung zu tun hat.

Gesellschaften und Gruppen konstruieren ihre eigenen Wirklichkeiten. Diese Deutung der Wirklichkeit ist in der Regel an Autoritäten delegiert, an gesellschaftliche Eliten, die zugleich als Sinngebungsinstanzen fungieren. "Wirklichkeit" ist das, was Menschen wissen, erfahren, fühlen, was sie als eine Realität wahrnehmen. An ihr richtet sich Handeln aus. So wird man auch nach der geglaubten Wirklichkeit der Ethnie fragen können, denn sie schafft sich als Deutung und Begriff Realität.

II. Die Konstruktion der Ethnie

Wir haben das Ende des 18. Jahrhunderts als die Epoche des Beginns der liberalen, nationalen Bewegungen in Europa, der europäischen Aufklärung und der philanthropischen Pflicht zur Verbesserung des Menschengeschlechts bestimmt. Die Idee des Volksgeistes, wie sie Johann Gottfried Herder formuliert hatte, wäre eine humane, fortschrittliche Idee gewesen. Sein "Volksgeist" hatte jeder Ethnie nicht nur Eigenart sondern vor allem auch Eigenwert attestiert. Die Rolle, die Herders Gedanken in der Folgezeit gespielt haben, sind kaum zu unterschätzen. Sie haben besonders bei der schmalen Schicht der Intelligenz von Völkern ohne staatliche Organisation Resonanz gefunden. Eines dieser Völker sollten übrigens bald auch die Deutschen sein, die seit 1806, dem Ende des Heiligen Römischen Reiches Deutscher Nation, in einem zwar weitgehend sprachlich und kulturell, aber nicht mehr und noch nicht politisch geeinten Lande lebten und sich seither mit ihrer Identität schwer taten. Eine Wende in Herders Denken ist offenbar: 1787 hieß es noch "Stimmen der Völker in Liedern", ganz im Sinne des pluralistischen Ansatzes; 1805 waren es dann in verengter nationaler Perspektive "Deutsche Volkslieder".

Johann Gottfried Herder war im 18. und mehr noch im 19. Jahrhundert, in den national unerlösten Völkern Europas hoch verehrt. Auch Jacob Grimm hatte Kontakte mit und

Wirkung in Finnland und Serbien. Vuk Stefanović Karadzić, "Onkel Vuk", nutzte dieses Vorbild. Utješenović machte etwas später schon deutlicher gegen die schnelle Modernisierung Front, als er sich über die Hauskommunion der Slaven äußerte und dabei ausdrücklich auf Wilhelm Heinrich Riehls sozialen Konservatismus Bezug nahm. Herder wurde als der gelesen, der jeder Ethnie nicht nur eine Seele als eigenen Ausdruck zugesprochen hatte, sondern als politische Konsequenz das Recht auf eigene territoriale Staatlichkeit. Herder, Grimm und Riehl sind Ahnen unseres Faches und gleichzeitig der Geschichte einer auf Ethnizität gegründeten Legitimität der europäischen Völker. Für die "jungen Staaten" der dritten Welt bietet die Völkerkunde heute "die einzige Möglichkeit zu ihrer Rekonstruktion. Sie ist... so etwas wie eine 'nationale Geschichtswissenschaft' und in zunehmendem Maße unentbehrlich für ihr Selbstverständnis" (Nachtigall: 136). Schon deshalb gab und gibt es eine Zuständigkeit auch der europäischen Ethno-Wissenschaften, weil sie am Entdeckungsprozeß und an den Deutungen des Ethnischen beteiligt waren. Wissenschaftsgeschichte ist mit der Geschichte der Gesellschaften eng verknüpft. Herders Ideen zum "Volk" werden heute grausam exekutiert, nicht nur in den zerfallenden Reichen Ost- und Südosteuropas, sondern auch in den reichen Industrieländern des Westens. Die ethnokulturellen Konflikte werden – wenn es gut gehen wird – neue, kleinere territoriale Einheiten als Lösungen zeitigen. Das Gesetz der "wachsenden sozialen Einheiten" (Mühlmann, 191 ff.), das von den Stämmen zu den Völkern und den Einheitsstaaten führte, scheint fragwürdig geworden. Die Nationalstaaten beginnen sich, scheinbar spielerisch zuerst, in kleine Völker zu atomisieren, zu tribalisieren.

Alle Volksforscher wollten verändern und nahmen Maß an der Vergangenheit. Vergangenheit, das war immer die bessere Kultur mit der größeren, früheren, nun verlorenen Bedeutung. Damit mag es zusammenhängen, daß die Volkstumswissenschaften insbesondere in Ländern mit fragwürdiger oder bestrittener, behinderter, gefährdeter, noch nicht erreichter, oder noch nicht formulierter nationaler Definition ihre imposantesten Ausmaße annahm. Hier zitierte man in sinfonischer Musik und klassischem Tanz mehr als anderswo Folklore-Elemente. Kein Wunder, daß Jacob Grimm aus Deutschland seine Briefe wohl nach Finnland und Serbien, nach Dänemark und Schweden, nicht aber nach Frankreich und England schickte. Länder mit hochentwickelter Volkskunde, so könnte man vereinfachen, gehörten zum Kartell der Getretenen. Wo die nationalpolitische Identität unbezweifelt war, brauchte es die scheinbare Bescheidenheitswissenschaft nicht. Was sie hätte leisten können, war anderweitig längst durch Demokratie oder Industrie abgedeckt.

Der Begriff der Ethnie hat zu Beginn der europäischen Moderne einen spezifischen Akzent und eine beschreibbare Funktion erhalten. Die Volkstumswissenschaften können so als die eigentlich modernen Wissenschaften verstanden werden. Ihre Entstehung gehört zur Geschichte der modernen bürgerlichen Gesellschaften. Ihre Leistung besteht darin, für eine zunehmend undurchschaubar werdende Welt mit der Kategorie "Ethnie" ein ordnende Struktur zu schaffen.

Mohammed Rassem hat vor über 40 Jahren auf einen Zusammenhang der Volkstumswissenschaften mit dem Etatismus des 18. Jahrhunderts hingewiesen (Rassem). In der Phase der Ablösung der kleineren altständischen, gemeinschaftlich organisierten Einheiten durch ein einheitliches staatliches Territorium erklärt sich die Notwendigkeit einer neuen Kategorie: Die Abstraktion "Staat" bedarf einer neuen Idee der Verbindung. Der rationale moderne Staat verwandelt sich (jedenfalls im Einflußbereich dieses Denkens) durch eine scheinbar naturwissenschaftliche, aber gleichzeitig und vor allem emotionale Kategorie, die Ethnie (und später die "Rasse"), zur Abstammungsgemeinschaft. Die "natürlich" begründete Vorstellung von der Gemeinsamkeit füllt die rationale Vergesellschaftung mit dem emotionalen Kitt der Ethnie als Bindemittel. Die behauptete Abstammungsgemeinschaft imitiert eine Familienbeziehung und einen exklusiven Gemeinsamkeitsglauben. Diese moderne Verwandtschaft der Ethnie wird zur geglaubten Wirklichkeit, indem der Ideologie eine emotionale Struktur eingezogen wird, die eine neue, nationale Erfahrung ermöglicht. Krieg, aber auch Geschichte, Literatur und Volksdichtung werden zu Verständigungsmustern der Ethnien, weil in ihnen Gemeinsamkeit erfahrbar wird. Das Ethnische ist eine Antwort auf die Auflösung der traditionalen Strukturen.

Die Ethnien aber sind nicht naturgewachsen, sondern sie sind im intellektuellen Diskurs im Verlauf der Modernisierung hergestellt worden. Es ist deshalb wichtig, den historischen Punkt zu bestimmen, an dem die Ethnie, als Abstammungsgemeinschaft und als Blutsverwandtschaft interpretiert, in die Erfahrung der Menschen eingedrungen war. Die Ethnie bestimmt die Konstruktion einer neuen Wirklichkeit.

Jede Gruppe von einiger Geschlossenheit, jedes Individuum, denkt ethnozentrisch. Weltbild und Weltdeutung nehmen die eigenen Kulturzustände und die Sozialstruktur als die einzig natürlichen an. Immer wird das Eigene erst in der Auseinandersetzung mit dem Fremden denkbar. Das Selbstverständliche kann in seiner Selbstverständlichkeit ohne das Fremde nicht einmal gedacht werden. Erst der Versuch der Unterscheidung (die Suche nach Identität) löst Definitionen aus. Die Überschreitung des ethnozentrischen Horizonts stellt die eigenen Selbstverständlichkeiten in Frage und führt zu einem theoretischen Interesse, das in die Ethnowissenschaften mündet. Der Prozeß der Verwissenschaftlichung unseres Alltags ist also gebunden an eine faktische Horizonterweiterung.

An die Stelle des persönlichen Suchens nach einem individuellen Lebensentwurf, wie ihn die Aufklärung vorgesehen hatte, wird die Idee der Ethnie als einer neuen Lebensgemeinschaft gesetzt. Sie widerruft die Aufklärung und nimmt ein vorliegendes Muster auf, das auf der Basis der Idee der gemeinsamen Abstammung neu begründet wird. Dabei nimmt dieses Muster an kleinen, exotischen und binnenexotisch-europäischen Naturvölkern (z.B. Hirten) Maß. War der Begriff der Ethnie für die außereuropäischen Völker vorbehalten gewesen, so werden nun die eigenen Volkskulturen wie Stammesgesellschaften in Hochkulturgesellschaften verstanden. In der Ethnie sollen die bislang gültigen, sozialen Herkunftsunterschiede, wie sie rechtlich fixiert waren (etwa für die Zulassung zum Handwerk), durch die Gemeinsamkeit der nationalen Abstammung überspielt werden. In der Idee der Ethnie steckt anfangs also auch ein demokratisches Moment, allerdings mit nationaler Exklusivität.

Was von den Sinngebungsinstanzen (Kirche, Staat, Politikern, Intellektuellen) gedeutet wird, formiert gesellschaftliche Erfahrung. Die Rationalität der ständisch-ökonomischen Einteilung der vorbürgerlichen Gesellschaft war als "natürlich", von Gott gegeben durch die alten Autoritäten gedeutet und auch so erfahren worden. Gilde, Zunft, Hausgemeinschaft, Bauernschaft und Dorfgemeinschaft waren selbstverständliche und nicht zu hinterfragende Sozialitäten gewesen. Der moderne Staat und der sich beschleunigende Wandel zerstören sie, wiewohl man einige weiter propagiert.

Von der Entdeckung oder gar der Erfindung der Ethnie zu reden, macht nur vor diesem Hintergrund und nur dann Sinn, wenn darin ihr "künstlicher" Charakter zum Ausdruck kommt. Der Hinweis auf die "Erfindung der Tradition", von Eric Hobsbawm formuliert, läßt sich als eine spezifische Nutzung des Historischen in der Moderne verstehen (Hobsbawm). Im Ethnischen ist eine erzählte und höchst plausible Geschichte des Eigenen enthalten. Die eigene Kultur wird ethnisiert, naturalisiert und später biologisiert.

Der Volkskundler Ernst Klusen hatte das Verhältnis von Wirklichkeit und Deutung am Beispiel des Volkslieds mit "Fund und Erfindung" (Klusen) gekennzeichnet. Er hatte damit eine charakteristische Situation am Beginn der Moderne und gleichzeitig am Beginn des "romantischen" Zweiges der Ethno-Wissenschaften beschrieben, die sich anfangs ausschließlich der mündlichen Traditionen annahmen. Das 19. Jahrhundert wurde so für unser Fach zur philologischen Epoche. In der Sprache wurde der "Samen für die Zukunft" (Jacob Grimm) in den nur sprachlich, aber nicht politisch geeinten Völkern gesehen; keine andere Wissenschaft schien so sehr dem

Nationalen verpflichtet wie die Sprachwissenschaften.

Bei der Erforschung von Lied, Sage und Märchen ging man von der Voraussetzung aus, in den treu von Mund zu Mund getragenen Überlieferungen der Bauern sei – ohne die Einmischung von Fremdem wie bei der an Frankreich orientierten Kultur der Bürger – der Ursprung des Nationalen zu finden. Auf diesen Ursprung kam es an; in ihm war die Ethnie noch unzerteilt, gemeinschaftlich, ganz bei sich. Volk und Ethnie sind damit auch Kategorien des Widerstands gegen die Moderne, sie sind Ausdruck der Verweigerungen und Protest gegen die Auflösung der traditionellen Strukturen, Protest auch gegen die Unübersichtlichkeit. In ihnen versucht man, Fließendes zu fixieren. Die Wissenschaft Volkskunde hält die Dinge fest, konserviert ihr "Wesen". Kultur wird auf dem Status quo gehalten; Volkslied, Märchen und Sage kommen zu ihrem "Wesen".

Damals war etwas als Volkslied entdeckt worden, was vorher ganz selbstverständlich schon gesungen worden war, ohne aber eigens thematisiert zu sein. Was für ein Wandel in der Wahrnehmung und Deutung durch die Gebildeten! Plötzlich galten die Gesänge der Landleute, die man vorher eher mit dem Grunzen der Schweine verglichen hatte (so, wie man die Bauern selbst eher den Tieren zuordnete und nicht bei seinesgleichen sah), als Ausdruck der Volksseele. Da die Volksseele im nationalen Kontext als eine sakrale Angelegenheit aufgefaßt worden war, mußte ihr Ausdruck, der Gegenstand Volkslied, heilig sein. Das Volkslied wurde auf eine sakrale Ebene gehoben, es bekam sein "Wesen", von dem man behauptete, es sei dauerhaft, reiche aus der Frühzeit her, sei unveränderlich, sei national. Diese neue Bestimmung des Volksliedes führte dazu, daß das Derbe, Obszöne und Böse in ihm keinen Platz mehr haben konnte. Der als ethnisch-national bestimmte Gesang, der Ausdruck der Volksseele, sollte auf dem Altar des Nationalen niedergelegt werden können. Dazu mußten die Gesänge veredelt und notwendigerweise vom tatsächlich gesungenen Lied abgesondert werden. Es entstand also mit dem Volkslied eine neue Kategorie Lied, die es so vorher nicht gegeben hatte, ein Produkt der nationalen Identitätsfabrik. Die ausgewählten Lieder, veredelt, gereinigt, nationalisiert, sollten dem Volke wiedergeschenkt werden. Das Geschenk sollte neue, edle Menschen schaffen. Ein neues Volk sollte durch die "ethnisch" definierten Lieder entstehen.

III. Die Verwissenschaftlichung der Alltage

Die Erfindung der Ethnie läßt sich an den Beginn der Moderne setzen, oder, anders gesagt, an den Beginn neuer Strukturen, die von der Gemeinschaft zur Gesellschaft führen. Sie führen von der täglich erfahrenen und in ihrer Wirklichkeit überprüfbaren Gemeinschaft, bei der man einen großen Teil der Angehörigen kennt, zur abstrakten Gesellschaft des modernen Staates. Das Ende der alten Ordnungen und Einteilungen macht es notwendig, Gemeinsamkeiten für die neue, unüberschaubare Großgemeinschaft "Staat" zu suchen. An die Stelle der praktikablen und tatsächlich erfahrbaren Gemeinschaft tritt nun der nicht mehr erfahrbare, unübersehbare Staat als ethnische "Familie". Jedes Mitglied dieser Familie trägt Verantwortung auch für die ihm nicht persönlich bekannten Verwandten. Der Staat wird zu einer Herkunftsgemeinschaft, die von ihren Deutern mit "kollektiver Erinnerung" ausgestattet wird. Hier beginnt eine literarisch vermittelte Produktion von Erinnerungsgeschichten der Ethnie, die als "kollektive Erinnerung" individuelle und auf eigene Erfahrung gegründete Erinnerung immer wieder überdeckt. Die Ethnologen sind die neuen Geschichtenerzähler (Köstlin).

Wie das Volkslied, so konnten diese Geschichten nur am fiktiven Anfang, im nationalen Ursprung gefunden werden. Dieser mußte freigelegt werden. Denn das Ethnische mußte ein Allgemeines sein, wenn es als gemeinsames Vielfaches für alle Mitglieder der Gesellschaft brauchbar sein sollte. Es sollte alle geforderten Eigenschaften enthalten, die für den Aufbau der Nation nützlich waren. Die Deutungswissenschaften haben die Differenzen betont, das Unterschiedliche akzentuiert und dazu beigetragen, die Unterschiede zur Erfahrung werden zu lassen. Ethnische Identität ist durch Differenz hergestellt worden.

So wie sich das Volkslied vom alltäglich gesungenen Lied entfernte, um dann als veredelte Inkarnation des Nationalen dienen zu können, mußte auch das Ethnische von seiner Wirklichkeit abgehoben, entfremdet werden. Es handelte sich um eine Selektion positiver Eigenschaften, die dabei entstanden waren. Die Lieder galten als heilige Sprachdenkmäler und waren doch mehr. Sie wurden, und wiederum kann man sagen, auf einmal, zum Gegenstand der nationalen Wissenschaften. Es waren neue Wissenschaften, die das Nationale (von lat. nasci = wachsen) oft erst herzustellen suchten. Wo dieses Nationale bereits geklärt war, wie etwa in Frankreich, brauchte es – wie oben angemerkt – diese Wissenschaften auch nicht. Wann hätte man dort den Bauern verklärt?

Das Eigene wie das "Andere", das Verfremdete wie das angeblich "Echte", bedurften der Interpretation, der Deutung. Die Deutung übernahmen, als neue Sinngebungsinstanzen, die entdeckenden und dann das Entdeckte beschreibenden Institutionen der Wissenschaft. Wichtig ist, daß die Deutungen der Wissenschaft auf die Dauer nicht ohne Einfluß auf die Lebenswirklichkeit der "einfachen Menschen" bleiben konnten. Richard Weiß hat einmal angemerkt, daß bei den Schweizer Hirten die Fremdverklärung (durch Rousseau und andere) bald in heilsame Selbstverklärung umgeschlagen sei (Weiß).

Die Wissenschaften bestimmen seitdem auch den Alltag der Menschen. Wo selbstverständliche Orientierungen angesichts der behaupteten Komplexität der Welt nicht mehr ausreichen, sind Orientierungswissenschaften gefragt, die Wissen produzieren. Wollte man die bis heute damit verbundenen Deutungen knapp formulieren und verdichten, dann steht auf der einen Seite das Zeitalter der Dauer und der göttlich legitimierten, "natürlichen" ständischen Gliederung, in die man hineingeboren wurde: Hausgemeinschaft, Nachbarschaft, Markgenossenschaft, Dorf, Zunft, Gilde, Rache- und Rechtsgemeinschaft, Minderheit oder Mehrheit, Privilegiertheit und Nichtprivilegiertheit von Völkern, Gruppen, Mann und Frau. In der Dorfgemeinschaft mit egalitärer Landzuteilung ohne Privateigentum unter den Berechtigten gab es eine allgemein akzeptierte Hierarchie der Welt, wie sie sich in der Sitzordnung in der Kirche, in Kleidung und in der Alltagserfahrung abbildete. Es war die erfahrene Ordnung, die, ideologisch gestützt durch die aus dem Mittelalter hereichende Weltdeutung der analogia entis, der Abbildhaftigkeit alles Seienden, als populäres, hängengebliebenes Wissen in die Neuzeit getragen worden war. Dies war die Ordnung der Welt. Die 'auctoritas', die Urheberschaft, die Autorität dieser Ordnung lag bei Gott.

Das traditionale Leben wird – und das ist die andere Seite – in der Moderne abgelöst durch eine neue Deutung der Welt. Sie ist für die neuen Deutungsmächte spätestens seit der französischen Revolution durch die am eigenen Leib erfahrene Bewegung in der Gesellschaft und die Auflösung traditioneller Bindungen markiert. Hier ist nichts mehr fest, hier gehört nichts mehr zusammen und umsomehr will befestigt werden – es muß homogenisiert werden, was nicht mehr zusammenpaßt. Ethnographien sind Homogenisierungswissenschaften. Sie markieren eine neue Rolle der Wissenschaft, die für den Alltag der Menschen eine Bedeutung bekommt. Insofern können sie als Markierung der Trennung zweier Epochen dienen. Geistes- und gesellschaftsgeschichtlich entstehen sie an der Grenze zwischen dem Denken der altständischen Gesellschaft in natürlichen, gottgegebene Ordnungen und einer europäischen Modernität, die bis dahin auch von den neuen bürgerlichen Deutungseliten noch nicht geahnt werden konnte. Die wissenschaftliche Kategorie Ethnie wird eine Denkfigur zur Bewältigung der Modernität.

Der Begriff der Ethnie steht damit auch am Anfang einer Entwicklung der Wahrnehmung der Welt, die immer weniger durch Erfahrung und immer mehr durch wissenschaftliche Deutungen geprägt ist. Die Ethnie, in der das "Wesen" des Volkes aufbewahrt ist, bekommt "Dauer" attestiert, Kontinuität, soll ewig gleich bleiben. Ein Bedarf an gesellschaftlicher Homogenisierung fußt auf den Erfahrung eines verlorenen Zusammenhangs des Selbstverständlichen. Der Zerfall der Selbstverständlichkeiten (der für sich schon "Deutung" ist), wird zum Auslöser dieser neuen Argumentationsfigur "Ethnie". Sie bildet zum Ende des 18. Jahrhunderts im Rahmen des europäischen Etatismus die Ethnowissenschaften aus. Diese sind Staats-Wissenschaften, die sich bemühen, das Rationale irrational auszugestalten und einen Mythos zu etablieren, der die neue Gemeinschaft "Staat" schafft. In ihm, als einer fiktiven Familie, sollen die Menschen glauben, daß sie durch gemeinsame Ahnen verbunden sind. Damit wird das Projekt der Moderne, das der Staat als "Gesellschaft" darstellt, widerrufen. In der Ethnie, im "Volk" wird eine neue Erfahrung der Gemeinschaft hergestellt, die ethnisch gedeutet wird und die Menschen im Abstraktum Staat homogenisieren soll.

Die Entdeckung der Ethnie findet in der Schichten und Klassen überwölbenden Idee der Nation (und hier sind Ethnie und Nation austauschbar) ihre Erfüllung. Die Ethnie hebt freilich auf, was eben noch aufklärerisch geöffnet schien. An die Stelle des persönlichen Suchens nach einem eigenen, autonomen Lebensentwurf wird das Subjekt in eine neue Gemeinschaftsform eingeschmolzen: in die Ethnie. In ihr kennt man den Einzelnen nicht mehr. Die Ethnie überspringt soziale Herkunftsunterschiede durch nationale Kultur.

Die Ethnie wird so zur Summe der Gemeinsamkeitsgeschichten. Die "Erfindung" der Ethnie gleicht der Konstruktion einer gemeinsamen Familiengeschichte (wie wir sie von den mittelalterlichen Herrscherfamilien kennen), die sich auf Blutsverwandtschaft gründet. Die Ethnie ist damit zugleich auch die entschiedene Absage an die traditionelle, korporationsrechtliche Wahlverwandtschaft. An deren Stelle tritt eine schicksalhafte, biologisch-naturwissenschaftliche Deutung der Gemeinsamkeit. Sie ist der Preis für die größere Gemeinschaft "Staat". Damit wird "ethnisches" Verhalten, gut oder böse, zur "Natur", unausweichlich und gerechtfertigt. Geschichte als ethnische Natur bestimmt die Menschen.

Man könnte fragen, wie es dazu gekommen war, daß Gruppen unterschiedlicher Sprache und Konfession, vielleicht auch unterschiedlichen Aussehens, die jahrhundertelang einigermaßen friedlich nebeneinander gelebt, also "Interethnik" praktiziert hatten, diesen Zustand auf einmal für unerträglich hielten, sich von ihren bisherigen Nachbarn durch Grenzen trennen und nur noch unter sich sein wollten. Dies ist nicht ohne die bürgerlichen Vordenker, die Gründerväter unserer Wissenschaft geschehen. Volkskunde ist von ihrem Anfang an eine Deutungswissenschaft des Ethnischen gewesen. Ihre Projektionen trugen dazu bei, die europäischen Territorien, in denen Vielsprachigkeit und Multikulturalität die Regel waren, zuerst zu Nationalstaaten mit dem Herrschaftsanspruch der dominierenden Schicht zu machen, und dann, in einem zweiten Schritt, die regionalen Besonderheiten als "kulturelle Vielfalt" im Regionalismus des 19. Jahrhunderts gegen den Anspruch der Metropolen zu setzen.

Max Weber hatte die Ethnie dahingehend bestimmt, "daß sie eben an sich nur (geglaubte) Gemeinsamkeit, nicht aber Gemeinschaft" (Weber: 237 f.) sei; sie sei "nur ein die Vergemeinschaftung erleichterndes Moment". Er hat damit eine "künstliche" Art der Entstehung der Ethnie beschrieben. Die "Lebensführung des Alltags" sei es, und Dinge, die sonst "von untergeordneter sozialer Tragweite erscheinen", die zur "ethnischen' Scheidung" dienen. Sie freilich sind relativ beliebig.

IV. Die Gründerzeit

Das Ende des 19. Jahrhunderts darf als Gründerzeit der ethnographisch-volkskundlichen Wissenschaften bezeichnet werden. In Europa etablierten sich volkskundliche Institutionen. Wissenschaftliche Gesellschaften und Vereinigungen wurden in Wien, Stockholm, Kopenhagen, Berlin oder Budapest gegründet. Die wissenschaftlichen Gesellschaften edierten Zeitschriften. Die nationalen Museen für Volkskunde und nur 10 Jahre später auch die regionalen Volkskundemuseen verdanken ihre Entstehung nicht so sehr dem Interesse am Volk und seinen Lebensbedingungen, das Interesse galt vielmehr einem Substrat. Im Grunde hatte sich seit dem Beginn des 19. Jahrhunderts prinzipiell nicht viel geändert –

bis auf eines: dieses Interesse am Volk war in der Breite der Bürgermilieus populär geworden. Es konnte einem vielfach instabilen, desorientierten, jedoch zahlenmäßig größer gewordenen Bürgertum als Fluchtpunkt dienen. Denn die Definition des Eigenen, das verloren zu gehen drohte, unterlag der sichernden Musealisierung. Die fiktive Volksgeschichte wurde von Fachleuten gedeutet und in den bürgerlichen Blick auf das Land eingebettet.

Am Beginn der volkskundlichen Institutionen jener Zeit stehen Vereinigungen, deren Mitglieder nicht Fachleute im engeren Sinne waren. Erst in der nächsten Generation traten akademische Spezialisten auf den Plan. Die Volkstumswissenschaften waren nun eine öffentliche Angelegenheit geworden. Das ethnographische Paradigma substituierte das Nationale. Die bäuerlich-agrarische Herkunft der Einwohner, bunt, stark, vielfältig ausgestaltet, erdverbunden und traditionell-konservativ, wurde zum Ausgangspunkt und Sammelplatz in den nationalen Kulturen gemacht. In pompösen Milleniumsfeiern zelebrierte etwa das junge Bürgertum Ungarns das Recht auf seine folklore-ethnische Herkunft. Der ethnographische Teil der Milleniumsausstellung war weit größer ausgefallen als bei vergleichbaren Ausstellungen anderswo. János Janko hatte ein vielbewundertes Dorf mit 26 Bauernhäusern und Nebengebäuden aus verschiedenen Gegenden Ungarns komponiert. Das Dorfbild zeigte sich als Symbol der Verschmelzung, als Abbild des großen Ungarn, das im Dörflich-Ethnischen friedlich vereint war. Auf diese Weise wurde Gesellschaft durch ihre Herkunft homogenisiert. Ähnliche Bezüge hatte Artur Hazelius schon im schwedischen Skansen dargestellt. Genau zu diesem Zeitpunkt kündigt sich überall das Ende eben dieser bäuerlichen Welten an. Die Folklorisierung einer Sache wird erst in ihrem Niedergang möglich, wenn bisherige Selbstverständlichkeiten ihr Ende finden.

Über das Ende des 19. Jahrhunderts wissen wir mehr, seit wir die Geschichte unserer Disziplin historisieren und sie mit der Gesellschaftsgeschichte verzahnen. So erfahren wir etwa, daß "Volkskunst" nicht in der Zeitlosigkeit der Bauernkulturen existierte, sondern als Begriff mit der Modernisierung verbunden ist. Die Rede über "Volkskunst" schiebt das Nationale bürgergerecht in einen (vor allem) ästhetischen Diskurs, in dem "Volkskunst", als "Husfliden" in den skandinavischen Ländern, zu einem nationalen, aber ausreichend breit gefächerten Stil wird. Diese Entscheidung fällt spät. In den Kunst- und Gewerbemuseen waren bereits seit den 1860er Jahren die historischen Stile längst und bis zum Überdruß durchgespielt worden. Die Mustersammlungen waren ausgebeutet, auch die orientalischen Stile, vom Maurischen bis hin zum Chinesischen und Japanischen, hatten sich erschöpft. Als die Vorbildsammlungen einem desorientierten Handwerk nichts mehr zu bieten hatten, wurde Volkskunst als Stil entdeckt und an die Historismen angehängt. So beginnt im Historismus ein Verfahren, das Stil und Ästhetik im Zentrum sieht und der Postmoderne ähnelt. Das Zitieren historischer Stile und der Verweis auf das Historische wie die Mischung des Historischen mit dem Exotischen erinnern an gegenwärtige Praxen. Das Zitat des Echten war zur Signatur und zur kulturellen Technik der ästhetischen Produktion geworden.

Der Kunsthistoriker im Wiener Kunstgewerbemuseum, Alois Riegl, wollte "Volkskunst, Hausfleiß und Hausindustrie" noch 1895 als regionale Hausproduktion dezentral vor Ort lassen. Er hatte damit insbesondere ein Problem der Flächenstaaten im Auge. Auf diese Weise sollte der Zuzug der Landbevölkerung in die explodierenden Großstädte gebremst werden. Dieser demographische Aspekt, später Merkantilismus und moderne Gewerbeförderung in einem, verband sich mit der Akzentuierung des Ethnischen, des Grundmusters der nationalen Kultur. Sie war (nicht bei Riegl) von "Fremdlingen" zu säubern. Josef Pommer, der Propagandist des Deutschtums im Volkslied Österreichs, spricht 1902 von "Schädlingen", vor denen das Lied zu schützen sei. Das ist schon die Sprache und das Denken des Ratlosen, die kein anderes Argument mehr auszuspielen vermag und im ästhetischen Felde die "ethnische Säuberung" verlangt.

Man muß sich die Situation der verschreckten Bürger vor Augen halten, die am rapiden Wandel, am rasanten Aufstieg der Industrie und am Wachstum der Städte kaum aktiv, sondern eher begleitend und (meist kritisch) kommentierend teilnahmen. Wie beim Autofahren muß, wer das Fahrzeug lenkt, keine Angst davor haben, daß ihm Geschwindigkeit und Kurven Unwohlsein und Übelkeit bereiten. Mitfahrern droht dieses Ungemach leicht, weil sie den Zumutungen nicht gewachsen sind, es sei denn, sie legten die Bremse ein. Als dieses Ritardando, als diese Bremse fungieren das ethnographische Paradigma und die Wissenschaft Volkskunde, die es erfindet und vertritt. Natürlich basteln in der nationalen Identitätsfabrik alle humanistischen Wissenschaften mit; sie alle erzählen nun ethnisch kolorierte Geschichten und binden sie in ästhetischen Kategorie ein.

Über ästhetische Kategorien wird geklärt, welche Menschen schön sind und welche häßlich, welche Musik, welche Landschaft, welche Malerei, welche Architektur. 1895 erscheint ein Buch mit dem Titel "Deutsches Volkstum". In ihm ist alles ethnisch grundiert, ob deutsche Tonkunst, deutsche Malerei oder deutsche Baukunst. Vor diesem Hintergrund bildet sich die Ästhetik der nationalen Referenzlandschaften aus: in Ungarn die Puszta der Tiefebene, für das deutschsprachige Österreich die Alpen, für Bayern ebenso, für den Norden die Heide und das Meer. Die Schweden machen das bäuerliche Dalarna zu ihrer demokratischen Urheimat, die Norweger zelebrieren die bäuerlichen Talschaften oder werden wieder Wikinger. Aufs Ästhetische reduziert, werden die Zeichen der ethnisch genannten Kulturen auf ihre ästhetisch-symbolische Signatur reduziert; als Beispiel denke man etwa an die Neubewertung und Wiederaufnahme der Backsteinarchitektur in Nordeuropa. Identitäten werden auf Differenz gegründet.

V. Das ethnographische Paradigma am Ende des 20. Jahrhunderts

Was in der Volkskunst noch harmlos war, wird in der Gegenwart brisant. Wer die Kultur eines Volkes zerstört, nimmt ihm seine Geschichte und Tradition, unterhöhlt offenbar tatsächlich seine Identität. Die Serben beschießen die Symbole des Unterschiedes, die katholischen Kirchen der Kroaten. Sie zerstören damit "ethnische" Symbole (möglicherweise werden die Kroaten auf diese Weise frommer als sie je waren). Mitte November 1993 wurde die alte türkische Brücke von Mostar, die *stari most*, von kroatischen Granaten vollends zerstört. Sie galt als Symbol für die muslimische Kultur in Bosnien-Herzegowina. In einem Krieg der bisher etwa 200 000 Menschen das Leben gekostet hat, ließ die Zerstörung eines von der Unesco bestätigten Kulturdenkmals mehr aufhorchen als die Massaker. In Banja Luka sollen die bosnischen Serben die Reste von vier beschädigten Moscheen in die Luft gesprengt haben. In Nordbosnien sind über 90% aller katholischen Kirchen zerstört. Die Ehre der Menschen und die Kulturdenkmäler der Völker werden geschändet und manchmal hat man den Eindruck, als funktioniere das bei den Artefakten wirkungsvoller.

Im Jahre 70 zerstörten die Römer den Tempel der Juden. Das war der Beginn der Zerstreuung dieses Volkes. Im Jahre 1938 brannten in Deutschland die Synagogen und diese Feuer markierten den Beginn der Vernichtung der Juden. In Polen beließ man es später bei der Entweihung der Synagogen. Sie dienten als Lagerraum oder als Kino. Die Rede von den ethnischen Säuberungen weist, wenn man nach Vorbildern sucht, auf die nationalsozialistischen Vollzugsmeldungen, ein Ort sei "judenfrei". Als Folge des von Deutschland angezettelten Weltkriegs sind nach 1945 etwa 12 Millionen Deutsche aus Osteuropa vertrieben worden, wie es das Potsdamer Abkommen vorsah. Dahinter steckte nicht nur der Gedanke einer Bestrafung Deutschlands für das angerichtete Unheil, sondern auch nationale Überlegungen, die sich auf den Wunsch nach ethnischer Reinheit gründeten.

Das 20. Jahrhundert geht seinem Ende zu und nähert sich der Jahrtausendwende. Dabei zeigen sich sowohl in den Nationen Osteuropas wie auch in den Industrienationen verblüffende Parallelen und zudem Ähnlichkeiten mit dem Ende des 18. und des 19. Jahrhunderts: die Wiederkehr des Ethnographischen, des Archaischen, des Mythos ist angesagt; alle raunen vom Eigenen. Geschichte und Ethnizität spielen, eingebettet in Fortschrittsgläubigkeit und die Kritik dieses Fortschritts, eine neue Rolle, mit der so niemand gerechnet hatte. Am Ende des 20. Jahrhunderts schwindet das Interesse am eigenen Raum irritierenderweise nicht in dem Maße, in dem der Globus verfügbar zu werden scheint. Die Börsenkurse aus Tokio werden uns jeden Tag im Fernsehen präsentiert, als ob sie für uns von Interesse wären. Doch nur für wenige Menschen ist die Welt das Dorf, von dem Marshall McLuhan einmal gesprochen hatte. Die demokratisierenden Hoffnungen, die man an die modernen Kommunikationstechnologien geknüpft hatte, sind ebenso dahin wie der Glaube, daß die Verfügung über das gleiche Wissen auch zur Egalisierung der Menschen führen würde.

Statt dessen ziehen sich die benachteiligten Ethnien zurück, bleiben ausgeschlossen und behaupten wehrhaft ihr Territorium, manchmal sogar mit einem wirklichen Krieg. Immer wieder arbeitet solche ethnische Säuberung mit dem "Fremden" als Erklärungsmuster. Es ist das Fremdmachen des Anderen, das Reden vom Bösen, vom Ungeheuer, mit dem man nichts zu tun haben will. Die Technik ist einfach. Die posthume Distanzierung der Rumänen von ihrem Diktator trieb wilde Blüten. Der "geliebteste Sohn des Volkes" wurde nun in der Renasterea banateanu vom 14.01.1990 beschuldigt, fremden Blutes zu sein. Den einstigen Schuhmachersohn machten ethnologische Zuschreibungen zum tatarisch-zigeunerischen Mischling. Man entdeckt einen "mongolischen Schlitz in seinem Auge", "hervorstehende Backenknochen", "dicke Lippen", "große Hängeohren und einen heimtückischen Blick", schließlich zeige die "orientalische Prunksucht..., die ganze Sippe ist kein Zweig vom lateinischen Stamm".

Je komplexer ein System ist, desto anfälliger ist es, und desto notwendiger sind Strategien, die Komplexität zu harmonisieren. In komplexen Systemen aber gibt es "sub-systeme". Sie haben die Tendenz, sich abzugrenzen, sich unabhängig zu machen. Je komplexer die Weltgesellschaften (angeblich) werden, umso mehr scheinen die einzelnen Gebilde, Staaten und Ethnien, einer Gegenbewegung zu unterliegen. Um sich vor der Anfälligkeit der Gesamtsysteme zu schützen, grenzen sich die einzelnen Ethnien ab. Sie identifizieren sich nicht mit dem großen Ganzen, sondern mit dem kleinen überschaubaren Eigenen. Die anfangs integrative Kraft der ethnischen Bewegungen schlägt dann um in destruktive, nationalistische Isolation.

Die Betonung der Ethnie als Komplementärbegriff zur Nation hatte ja im Modell des 19. Jahrhunderts einmal dazu beigetragen, daß eine größere Gemeinschaft in der Form des Staates ihren inneren Frieden finden konnte. Mit der Ethnie setzte man dem liberalistischen Kapitalismus als "Kultur" etwas Gleichwertiges entgegen. Innerlichkeit, tieferer Sinn und "Identität" sollten verhindern, daß alles zur Ware wurde. Die "inneren" Werte wurden aus dem Ethnischen, Regionalen abgeleitet. Die Nationalität und die darin aufgehobene ethnische Vielfalt sollten das ökonomische Tauschprinzip in die Moral einer allgemeinen Gegenseitigkeit einbinden. Das Prinzip dieser Moral der Gegenseitigkeit war es, dem anderen, dem ethnisch verwandten, auch wenn man ihn nicht kannte, etwas zu geben, weil er zur selben Gemeinschaft gehörte.

Nation und Ethnie, nationale und ethnische Abschottung bieten auch heute auf den ersten Blick viele Vorteile. Sie erklären infrastrukturelle, ökonomische Schwierigkeiten als Folgen der Fremdherrschaft (Kolonialismus, internationale Konzerne, kapitalistische Länder, Währungsungleichheiten etc.). Das ist oft nicht falsch, ist aber dennoch eine undifferenzierte Entlastung. Die Realität wird damit nur verzerrt erklärt und die Lösung der inneren Probleme verhindert. Dadurch aber wird die völkische, nationalistische Bewegung verschärft und der Bedarf an ethnischer Identität verstärkt. Je mehr diese Bewegung mit sich selbst als Ethnie beschäftigt ist, je weniger sie über ihre selbstgemachten Grenzen hinaus kommuniziert, umso geringer wird ihre Fähigkeit, auf Entwicklungen von außen zu reagieren. Die Einwirkungen von außen treffen dann auf eine unvorbereitete Ethnie. Sie reagiert wiederum mit verstärkter Abgrenzung und aggressivem Chauvinismus. Diese Rückkoppelung macht die ethnischen Bewegungen so gefährlich. Früher wurden sie durch Kriege oder innere Zusammenbrüche gestoppt.

VI. Konturen einer Ethnologia Europaea

Die Fachleute für das Ethnische sind bestürzt. So hatten sie es nicht gemeint, als sie ethnische Kultur zum Thema machten. Die Rede vom kulturellen ethnischen Erbe reicht also weit zurück. Dieses Erbe entwickelt sich immer mehr vom Geschenk zu einer Hypothek. Ethnische Geschichten werden, als "kollektives Gedächtnis" bezeichnet, medial verbreitet. Inzwischen dominiert in der kollektivierten Geschichte das Ethnische die individuelle Biografie so sehr, daß persönliche Erfahrungen vergessen oder umgedeutet werden. Bei Befragungen im Nachkriegs-Deutschland haben viele Menschen erzählt und beschrieben, sie hätten früher mit Juden guten Kontakt gehabt und immer gute Erfahrungen gemacht. Das "kollektive Gedächtnis", das die Nazis den Menschen vor allem in der Bildersprache innerhalb kürzester Zeit implantiert hatten, summierte alle Vorurteile, reaktivierte ältere Bilder, überlagerte eigene, authentische Erfahrungen. Es handelte sich (wie so oft) um eine Neuetablierung dessen, was man dann als kollektives Gedächtnis pluralisierte. Dieses angeblich kollektive Gedächtnis führte zu einem radikalen Wandel des moralischen Selbstverständnisses in jener Epoche. Die Bedeutung des "kollektiven Gedächtnisses", das auch in den modernen Ethnowissenschaften hoch gehandelt wird, wäre deshalb kritischer, als gegenwärtig der Fall, zu befragen.

Eine Strategie, bei der die Volkskunde mithelfen könnte (und das hätte sie schon lange tun können), wäre die, zu zeigen, daß nationale Kulturen immer zusammengesetzte Kulturen sind. Fremdheit und Migrationen, auch Fremdenhaß und seine Folgen, hat es immer gegeben. Die Erfahrungen des Selbstverständlichen allerdings, die man damit gemacht hat, wurden vergessen, verleugnet, ausgeblendet, von den Deutern verändert und in das sogenannte kollektive Gedächtnis eingebrannt. Insofern kann ein erneuter Blick zurück, in andere Regionen und Zeiten nicht schaden. Sonst könnte es sein, daß die zusammengesetzten Kulturen, aus denen die modernen Nationen bestehen, wieder zerstört werden, weil Fremdheiten nun auch innerhalb des eigenen Landes verstärkt und dort aufgebaut werden, wo sie bisher nicht erlebt worden waren.

Alles, was wir Erfahrung nennen, folgt gesellschaftlichen Deutungsmustern. Eines dieser Deutungsmuster war das revidierte, und damit vermeintlich moderne Konzept von Heimat und Identität, von Regionalität und Territorialität in der Industriegesellschaft: je entwurzelter der Mensch sei, umso mehr steige sein Bedarf an Symbolen des Heimatlichen, wie sie der Folklorismus biete. Diese Argumentation ist inzwischen dabei, das zu zerstören, was sie schaffen will, Heimat. Die Rede von Heimat und Identität wird biologisiert und ethnisiert und liefert nun das Instrumentarium für die ethnische Säuberung. Johann Gottfried Herder, der liberale, moralische Aufklärer, der Prophet des Ethnischen, hatte – das war bereits erwähnt – jeder Ethnie eine Seele ("Volksseele") zugesprochen, einen Eigenwert, eine Identität (obwohl es das Wort noch nicht gab). Er hat nie gesagt, daß diese Identität nur in einem ethnisch homogenen, sterilen Territorium zu verwirklichen sei.

Volkskundler hätten also die Aufgabe, ein ethnographisches Paradigma zu entwickeln, das nicht nur mit äußerlichen Symbolismen verklammert ist. Wir gehören alle in der Tat längst elaborierten Individualkulturen an. Aber diese Individualitäten sind darauf angewiesen, ihre Unverwechselbarkeit mit massenkulturellen Mitteln herzustellen. Mit dem Anspruch nach Individualität (und der Folge der Vereinzelung) korrespondiert ein Bedürfnis nach bergender Homogenität. Die Eigenart dieser Individualisierung kann es sein, daß sie sich versichernd in die als homogen interpretierte Vergangenheit wendet. Für die Richtung dieser Deutung trägt auch die Volkskunde Verantwortung. Deshalb muß es auch möglich sein, daß moderne Lebensformen als modern untersucht und akzeptiert und nicht nur vor der Folie des Vergangenen in einer Verlustbilanz gewertet werden.

Andernfalls trüge die Volkskunde dazu bei,

gesellschaftliche Problemlagen bloß zu ethnisieren (also unzureichend zu erklären) und damit die rationale Sicht auf die Probleme zu verhindern. Zu fordern wäre also eine neue Aufklärung, die Ansprüche an die vorhandene Intelligenz der Menschen stellte. Sie sollte Identifikationsangebote nicht gerade auf der wohlfeilen Ebene der Ethnizität anbieten. Gerade die Fachleute für Ethnisches könnten ihren Beitrag dazu leisten.

Es ist heute selbstverständlich, die Geschichte der Wissenschaften und ihrer Begriffe nicht bloß als gegeben hinzunehmen. Wissenschaftsgeschichte und Begriffsgeschichte sind zum Gegenstand eigener und eingehender Erörterungen geworden. Das muß auch für den Begriff der Ethnie und des Ethnischen gelten. Daraus ergibt sich eine Verantwortung der Wissenschaft, die, auch um den Preis der Destruktion des Fachs, in die Dekonstruktion von Begriffen führen muß. Die Aufgabe könnte in einen Nachweis münden: Ethnisches ist ein Konstrukt, ist immer zusammengesetzte Kultur gewesen. Das Bild von der Homogenität der Ethnie entstammt einer Suche nach Orientierung in einer historischen Stufe der Gesellschaftsgeschichte. Wer also hat was, wann und in welchem Interesse als Ethnie markiert, bestimmt? Wer hat sie mit der Idee einer kulturellen Homogenität ausgestattet, die es nie gegeben hat und die nur vor dem Horizont der mit Schrecken entdeckten Vielfalt der Kultur im eigenen Land gedacht werden konnte?

So oder so ähnlich sollten die Fragen lauten. Die Rekonstruktion einer Begriffsgeschichte schließt immer auch die Infragestellung, die Dekonstruktion des Begriffes selbst ein. Erst nach der Dekonstruktion eines Begriffes wie dem der Ethnie können neue Muster formuliert werden, die historische Erfahrungen in neue Wirklichkeiten hinein entwickeln. Die gelehrten Konstrukte der vergangenen zwei Jahrhunderte hatten Praxisfolgen. Die Deutungen wurden geglaubt, nachgelebt und zu Erfahrung gemacht. Sie konstituierten ständig neue Wirklichkeiten – gute und schlechte, hilfreiche und zerstörende. Die Ethnie trägt ihre Geburtsmale vom Beginn der Moderne als Krücke der Orientierung.

Immer dann, wenn wir – wie gegenwärtig allerorten – die Bindestrich-Kulturen erforschen und damit auch erfinden, reifizieren wir den bürgerlichen Traum von der Homogenität einer Kultur. Homogen aber ist Kultur immer nur durch eine interessengeleitete Deutung, durch die die jeweilige Kultur besser handhabbar gemacht werden soll.

Literatur

Eric Hobsbawm: Inventing Traditions. In: Eric Hobsbawm/ Terence Ranger (Eds:) *The Invention of Tradition*. Cambridge 1989.
Konrad Köstlin: Folklore, Folklorismus und Modernisierung. In: *Schweizerisches Archiv für Volkskunde* 87 (1991): 46–66.
Ernst Klusen: *Volkslied. Fund und Erfindung*. Köln 1968.
Wilhelm Emil Mühlmann: Ethnologie. In: W. Bernsdorff: *Wörterbuch der Soziologie*. Frankfurt 1972.
Horst Nachtigall: *Völkerkunde*. Frankfurt 1974.
Mohammed Rassem: *Die Volkstumswissenschaften und der Etatismus*. Phil.Diss. Basel 1951.
Max Weber: *Wirtschaft und Gesellschaft*. Tübingen 1976 (Studienausgabe).
Richard Weiß: Alpiner Mensch und alpines Leben in der Krise der Gegenwart. In: *Die Alpen*, 1957: 209–224.

Summary

The breakup of ethnic movements in the past few years has been a kind of surprise for modern ethno-sciences which had handled the small sets of ethnicity mainly as colourful decorations of modernity in the western societies while they described ethnicity in the eastern block as deprived or suppressed and bound mainly to the artistry of state folklore ensembles.

The article tries to deal with different movements in using the ethnic paradigm throughout the history of modernity and the synchronously invented ethno-sciences. The use of ethnicity as a point of orientation seems to culminate especially at the turn of the centuries and in the so-called 'crisis'. Ethnicity promises a model which reduces complexity and confirms identity. Ethnic identity seems to offer a middle range identity concept: smaller than the world society but homogeneous and bigger than the pure and isolated individuality of man.

This could explain the fact that we observe ethnic movements not only in the former eastern block which has lost its structures but also in the western countries which obviously articulate a need of consensus and homogeneity which now seems to be gained by means of ethnicity. The article accentuates also scientific strategies around ethnicity and discusses the responsibility of the ethno-sciences in our days.

Politics, Culture and Social Symbolism
Some Remarks on the Anthropology of Eastern European Nationalism

Peter Niedermüller

> Niedermüller, Peter 1994: Politics, Culture and Social Symbolism. Some Remarks on the Anthropology of Eastern European Nationalism. – Ethnologia Europaea 24: 21–33.
>
> The main subject of this paper is the interpretation of emerging nationalism in post-socialist countries of Eastern Europe. The first part of the study describes the conception and apprehension of national culture characteristic of Eastern Europe since the late 19th century. The main direction of the argumentation is to emphasize the social, political, and ideological functions of this perception of nationality. The second part of the paper tries to characterize post-socialism through general cultural feeling of uncertainty, and argues that the "new" nationalism can be interpreted only as a manifestation of cultural fundamentalism typical for Eastern Europe as a therapy in the periods of pervasive political and social changes.
>
> *Professor Peter Niedermüller, Department of Communication, Janus Pannonius University, Ifjúság u. 6, H-7624 Pécs, Hungary.*

"The return of history is at the same time the return of the demons of nationalism, which we thought were buried a long time ago" (Rupnik 1990: 135). Jacques Rupnik's remark made some years ago gains new and increasingly alarming dimensions in the wake of the murders of "tribal wars" overwhelming Eastern Europe. And the fact behind this keen announcement – the revival of nationalism – needs explanation, of course. Why, and how could it happen that the post-socialist countries have seemingly fallen back into the nationalisms typical of the 19th century with all the brutality of the 20th century; how was it possible that democracy looming in the wake of the collapse of socialism has led to murders, violence, and wars all the way from the Adria to the Caucasus. Can one interpret this situation at all? Probably not, since it is difficult to speak about murders in scientific terms. Nevertheless, the expanding ethnic tensions, the wars of the Balkan and the Caucasus, the incapability to handle the situation and the consequent feeling of helplessness draws attention – at least of scientific research – significantly to something else, namely the other, more hidden forms of nationalism or rather the importance of their research as well.

Due to the brutality of local, ethnic wars, the associated rude nationalist ideologies, and the "philosophy" of the mass media common sense tends to regard nationalism as the manifestation of primitive political culture, or rather, generally the manifestation of some kind of social and/or cultural primitivism. In reality, however, the situation is much more compound, since nationalism and its manifestations in hidden or symbolic forms have become the most definitive or constitutive factor of the social and political changes in Eastern Europe. The queries of the present study are directed to this particular situation, i.e. the latent but still pervasive presence of Eastern European nationalism. This presence cannot be understood without discussing the historical constitution of nationalism. This is a process involving not only the historical, political, or ideological genesis of nationalism, but involving its symbolic structure as well. The starting point of this analysis can be, what has already been expressed by many others in many ways, that is, nationalism is not something that exists inherently or originally. Nationalism primarily is a construction filled up with symbolic contents created by a group of people for the sake of reaching political, social, or cultural purposes in a given historical context (Gellner 1983: 125). An anthropological interpretation of nationalism demands the interpretation of this process of construction, or rather of the functions of this construction (cf. Spencer 1990: 288); and is unable or unwilling to deal with the historical and politological dimensions of this field. Revealing the symbolic dimensions of nationalism demands primarily the interpretation of those categories and notions that constitute so to say the pillar of the conceptual system of Eastern European nationalism, that is, of national culture, the concept of cultural homogeneity, and a particular image of the past. Correspondingly, in the first part of the present paper I will analyze the concept of national culture and identity that emerged gradually from the first third of the 19th century, established at the turn of the century, and became dominant after the First World War – not from a historical point of view, rather with a concern to the cultural logic of this concept. Then I make an attempt to examine the way of how and in what forms this idea arose following the breakdown of socialism in Eastern and in Southeastern Europe.

Nation and national culture: conceptions and their cultural logic

Nation has been one of the most frequently used, analyzed and interpreted category of the political, social and social-scientific discourse since the end of the 18th century.[1] A significant number of scientific approaches to nation origins from the assumption that nation, national state is the inevitable, essential consequence of social, historical development; a specific feature of human history that is inherently connected to modernization and modernity (cf. Giesen 1991: 10; Greenfeld 1990: 549; Gellner 1983: 55). Nation in the last two centuries was posed as the unchallengeable, single form of social existence – for the political ideologies, as well as for the scientific and the common-sense knowledge of everyday life; seemed as some natural or social property, as the only possible "historical fate" (Mommsen 1987: 162), as a "God-given way of classifying men" (Gellner 1983: 48) – behind which there has always been some kind of "myth of origin". Thus, it is almost obvious, that in the political discourse of modernity, those political and cultural languages that see nation not as a motive of historical development, but rather some kind of metaphysical basis, "the basis of all historical events" (Estel 1991: 214), inhabit a significant place. The essence of perception of nation manifested in different historical, political, social, and cultural patterns. To draft generally and slightly simplified, there are two historical alternatives or two different political practices. On one hand, nations emerged that are characteristic rather of Western Europe, and are based on the political participation of citizens; on the other hand ideas of nation based on ethnicity and cultural determination appeared, that are characteristic of Eastern and Southeastern Europe (Hobsbawm 1991: 18–23). This latter idea of nation had and has presumed "objective" criteria, like e.g. common descent, common traditions, common religion, common language, and common culture. However, the real substance of nation is made up by a hardly identifiable subjective unity, collectivity, a "national spirit", "the desire for living together" (cf. Estel 1991: 214–215; Finkielkraut 1990: 24–40) that is concealed behind the objective features.

As far as we consider nation a historical formation, which can be described along objective and subjective criteria, then we are compelled to agree the assertions that see nation as a "cultural unit" (Weber 1979: 95), as an "imagined order" (Lepsius 1990: 233), or as an "imagined community" (Anderson 1983). These metaphors indicate an apprehension that nation, as one form of social coexistence can be grasped inasmuch as there exist collective practices and representations filled up with symbolic contents, through which a nation represents itself (Foster 1991: 239) and the fiction of nation as an imagined community appears (Mommsen 1987: 168–169; Bauman 1990: 153). Here the term "fiction" does not refer simply to the made-up, the false, the untrue, but involves the category of nation that has been *made* and *created*; it concerns the attitude of construction. Nation is not an inherently existing reality; it emerges always and in all historical situations through social and cultural mediums, and exists only as the result, and at the same time as the process of this constitution and construction (cf. Weber 1979: 493; Giesen 1991: 12; Hobsbawm 1991: 2223). This perception of nation is inseparable from the creation of "national reality", the interpretation of political and cultural strategies conveying symbolic contents and meanings of this reality; it is inseparable from national culture itself (Kaschuba 1993: 239).

Nation and national culture are inseparable categories that mutually constitute each other, since society, as a mass of people living together is filled up with symbolic contents by national culture; this way, society is transformed into "nation" by a defined cultural substrate (Giesen 1991: 10). The construction of national culture rested on folk culture, on a certain perception of folk culture[2] everywhere in Europe; the structure and the content of this relation has become a central theme of ethnographic, anthropological, and social-historical inquiries during the last decade. To summarize this discussion it may be stated that four fundamental types of this link between national and folk or peat culture can be distinguished in Europe:

(a) The first type – certainly I do not mean temporal priority – is represented by France, or rather by the attitude that is reflected in the title of Eugene Weber's famous book: "*Peasants into Frenchmen*". This approach is based on the profound difference between rural and urban population and reflects the "strangeness" of rural France. The nature of this relation is a kind of acculturation, whereas "urban" France "domesticates" the country; integrates local (provincial) cultures into the culture of modernity, the modern society; that is, the dominant elite culture colonialises rural France. In this case social and political integration accompanying economic modernization required a kind of cultural homogenization, and this homogenization manifested in the integration of "underdeveloped France" into modernity (cf. Weber 1979: 486–493).

(b) The next type can be best illustrated on the example of Sweden. The situation in Sweden was different in that peasant culture had preserved its symbolic autonomy, moreover, to a certain extent it was preserved as a kind of national tradition (remember the northern parts of Dalecarlia in the late 19th century for example). Yet still, Swedish national culture is not based on some kind of integration of folk or peasant culture; it is rather the emerge of the aspiring urban middle class from the turn of the century. That is to say, in the concept of Swedish national culture the symbolic sphere, the sphere of peasant culture is inseparably and simultaneously present; together with the sphere of actual or real cultural practice, the everyday life of urban middle class (cf. Löfgren 1989).

(c) A further type is represented by Germany. In the beginning of the 19th century, a novel interpretation of the category of "folk" emerged, that influenced the whole conception of nation and national culture. The nature of this change was that the notion of folk referred to a community expanding to, and encompassing everyone; which based on descent, and did not exclude anyone from this community because of one's descent, education, or social belonging. In the wake of this process, a new category, the category of "Germanness" (*Deutschheit*) appears, which roots in the concept of the "folk" but is not equal to it, and the aim of which category is including, not excluding. The fundamental significance of "folk" and "folk culture" is preserved, but is not at all exclusive (cf. Kaschuba 1993: 245–246).

(d) The last type is shown by the relation of folk and national culture, which is characteristic of the Eastern part of Central Europe, Eastern, and Southeastern Europe. The present paper deals only with the analysis of this latter type. In this case national culture is identical with folk culture, or rather with the image of folk culture, more precisely with a peculiar understanding of "popularism" – with exclusive validity. In Eastern and Southeastern Europe the distinctiveness of this relation meant that peasant culture did not bear significance in itself, in its historical reality; rather the views, ideas and convictions concerning folk culture widespread in the society became definitive and served as points of reference throughout the creation of the concept of national culture (cf. Hofer 1991). The ideological tie among folk culture, national culture and popularism is not very easily apprehendable. That is to say, the concept of popularism – based on imagined reality of folk culture, on national character, and on absolute belonging to the folk – appeared as the antipode of something in the cultural dichotomy of modernization in this region of Europe (cf. Köstlin 1984: 25); and represented a kind of ideal.

Due to this motive, the political, ideological and cultural concept of folk culture and popularism was enriched by an important symbolic dimension.

"In all cultures there is something more 'solid' and something more 'fluid'. Something that is brought, and then wasted by everydays; and something that is preserved as a common property through generations. The 'fluid' part is considered as everydays, the 'solid' as feast. The language of everydays is that of closeness, which connects us to our contemporaries; the language of feasts is that of the distance, which connects us to our predecessors. According to the extent one possesses the language of everydays and of one's contemporaries, is one part of a communicative society, according to the extent one possesses the language of feasts and of one's predecessors is one part of a cultural community" (Assmann 1991: 11).

This image of folk culture grafted on national culture fulfilled (and fulfills today) precisely the same function as the above mentioned "solidity", permanence, common property, feast in its symbolic sense, the language, the knowledge of which is indispensable for being a member of a cultural community. Folk culture was – in this perception of national culture – not a historically existing way of life; it functioned as an absolute and only point of orientation in sociocultural space. This way a kind of cultural community and ideology of popularism came into being, a member of which cannot be everyone naturally; the knowledge and the exclusive use of the adequate cultural language established a symbolic grid or raster which outlines the symbolic borders inside of the society automatically. This cultural language and this symbolic grid contributed to the structuring of societies the way, that – resulting from its own cultural logic – created the category of cultural otherness within one and the same culture. The cultural logic of popularism postulated the imagined reality of folk culture as an absolute point of reference and defined cultural differences in terms of this reference. In other words: the imagined reality of folk culture described and defined cultural otherness through exclusion of all kinds of other cultural strategies, as inherent and unchangeable strangeness; defined cultural differences in terms, and in the context of political, ideological, social relations as a "we/they" opposition. Cultural difference and "self-other relations are matters of power and rhetoric rather than of essence" (Clifford, 1988: 14, cf. Clifford 1983, 1986). James Clifford's statement is fitting here as well. To sum it up: in Eastern Europe national culture was not built on the historical reality of folk culture, but rather on its imagined reality; which later was claimed as the single authentic one. The feeling of belonging to a nation, national identity meant (and means even today) to belong to a symbolic construction, and disregarding the really existing cultural worlds.

Thus, national identity is primarily based on a reference to a cultural tradition, a cultural identity in this region; it is constructed in a field of tension between culture and politics (Giesen 1991: 13–15). However, this culturally defined identity does not refer to the cultural tradition of a concrete social group, a historically existing life-world, rather to a mental, psycho-cultural state, which Max Weber called an "imagined uniformity" (*geglaubte Gemeinsamkeit*, Weber 1922: 219). This term touches exactly the essence, namely the fact, that this uniformity in itself – at least from the point of view of political usefulness – is not a sufficiently enduring category; this collectivity and/or uniformity has to be established, has to be created (cf. Bauman 1990: 162). That this collectivity is not at all some "gift of nature" is shown well by the example of language as a group-symbol (cf. Steger 1987; Bausinger 1991); more explicitly by the categories of "common history" and "common culture". That is to say, these latter concepts cannot ignore the more and more obvious recognition of modern social sciences, that the categories of "common culture", "common history", "collective memory", etc. are of a very limited use. Not only because cultural differences between social groups are much more subtly patterned, much more subtly worked out than common sense supposed and politics and ideology presumed, but primarily because even social groups thought to be identical are not homogeneous; individuals always "stand at different positions", see events and the world from "different point of views", that is, they use different kind of "optics". I do not mean only social differences, which are present in each group, and their result, the diverge worldviews, but the diverge perceptions of the world, rooting in psychic states of age, sex, and of the individual. In other words, I refer to those various, socially, culturally and psychically determined modes of perception, with the help of which the individual is able to perceive and to acknowledge the world surrounding him, and the history constituting the frames of his life. In the above mentioned term from Max Weber the adjective *"geglaubte"* signifies too, that – in social and cultural respect – there are no authentic communities and uniformities (neither in the sense of *Gemeinschaft*, nor of *Gemeinsamkeit*); rather there is an inherent diversity, from which with the support of various symbolic instruments – for the sake of various political, social, and ideological aims – something "common" is created (cf. Marcus/Fischer 1986: 45–77; Knorr-Cetina/Grathoff 1988).

The main consequence of the notion of national culture widespread in Eastern and Southeastern Europe since the middle of the 19th century – which equalled the symbolically loaded category of popularism to the idea of national culture – was the establishment of symbolic borders, which are fundamental and even today have still perceivable consequences in these societies; symbolic borders, the primary function of which was opposing to and separating from others. Separation from others, based on the sacredness and the invulnerability of tradition and national culture, served as "the most significant symbolic regulator of social, political, and cultural life" (cf. Eisenstadt 1991: 29). First of all, resulting from the fact, that this collectivity constructed by national culture can be defined exclusively against something or someone; one characteristic of symbolic borders is that they settle unbridgeable abysses within the very same society. Cultural uniformity, the laying down, the definition, the hidden existence of symbolic borders, the idea of collectivity, and the consequent "comparison of different cultures" (cf. Kaschuba 1993: 246) – at least in Eastern Europe – meant the creation and the declaration of the overt or latent, direct or symbolic images of the enemies, set up a kind of modern political witch hunt; all these factors were – within this concept of national culture – inherently connected to the construction, and to the symbolization of enemies. This concept of national culture cannot exist without symbolic enemies; the imagined "we", and the symbolic "they" are ontologically coherent.

This notion of national culture certainly has a powerful integrative function as well. On the one hand, national culture facilitates the individuals on different levels of social structure the *recognition*: they all *belong* to the same community. On the other hand, it offers the individuals living in different social situations the *possibility*: they *may* all belong to the same community. Thus, national identity is theoretically optional, theoretically open. Nevertheless, this choice has a compulsory character: either "we", or "they"; moreover, openness is incidental and is of a limited validity, that is, it is open only if the "candidate" owns the adequate "features". That is to say, this concept of national culture always serves the same goal: it offers such constructed patterns of identity for the individual, behind which there are no real social, political and cultural background.

This concept of national culture, and national identity split the societies of Central and Eastern Europe after the First World War decisively. On the one side, there was the "national" part of the society where the members were connected not by actual social and sociological qualities, but by the symbolic web of "national". This web is woven by the concept, by the ideology of "popularism" to which ideology the image of history possessing a defined and exclusive authenticity belonged organically. On the other side there were all the outsiders, the strangers, who could not belong, or did not want to belong under this web. The popularism, the "picture" of national past served as a kind of identification. One who knows this picture, who is included in it, or has "acquaintances" or "relatives" in it, is part of the nation. The others are not.

Let us make the point here: national culture as such does not necessarily lead to nationalism. Yet still, the concept of national culture dominant in Eastern and Southeastern Europe did necessarily lead to nationalism(s), since the use, the symbolic manifestation, the declaration of national culture as a mental and political concept, occurred always against (cultural, political, social, ethnic, etc.) otherness. In this part of Europe, where after the First World War an explosive melting pot of political, social, ethnic, and cultural differences emerged, this concept of national culture was of a fundamental importance, rooting in everyday life, and was a determining factor from the point of view of political behaviour. How deep the roots of this view, of this "tradition" were, is shown well by the current situation of the post-socialist countries.

Nationalism and post-socialism: the past in the present or the present of the past

Besides the well-known political and economic level of the all-embracing social changes in Eastern Europe there is an another dimension which is constituted by the radical change of everyday life, the change of the cultural world of "ordinary people".[3] Several dimensions of this change can be grasped from which I wish to stress only one – the cultural order of socialism, which might be the most significant for the interpretation of reviving nationalism. The Eastern European socialism created not only one type of political and economic systems, but produced, constituted a cultural world as well; established the rules of living and communicating within this cultural world, and the various repertoires of behaviour, it set the "stages" of social life, worked out its cultural and social dramaturgy, etc. For ordinary people other possibility than accepting this world and these rules was not – and following from the logic of cultural worlds could not be – offered. Accepting a cultural world, a cultural system of rules equals to its internalization to a certain degree; that is, the cultural world and the system of rules of socialism became parts of individual lives and life-histories – totally independent of the particular individuals' commitments to socialist ideology. Confronting and turning against socialism politically, or – what was primarily specific of Hungary – resistance manifesting in the private spheres of life did not alter the cultural world itself: we all were partakers and at the same time we are inheritors and survivors of this world. Therefore attempts bearing political, ideological or other implications, directed to demolish this cultural world meant the symbolic annihilation of individual life-histories as well. Hardly can it be seen a coincidence that in the case of significant layers of the society, the political, social change of the system was accompanied by the experience of losing one's own history – here I stress again: independently of the individual ideological commitments. The breakdown of a familiar, accustomed cultural world in itself results in the loss of the identity which is especially the case when the collapse of a cultural world is not the consequence of inside moves or developments rather it is the result of the destructive effects of political and ideological motives. The struggle of post-socialist administrations, governments and ideologists to present the age of socialism as a "vicious era" lacking all positive values became a fundamental topic in ordinary people's increasing crises of identity. First of all because the experience of losing one's own history is accompanied by the questionability of the cultural knowledge used up to the given time, and of the further useability of this knowledge. Consequently, one becomes a stranger in one's own life-history, since what vanishes from behind individual actions is the history that had furnished the happenings of individual lives with meaning, as the single and sole authentic context. The only result of these politically motivated efforts is a crisis of identity, which more and more profoundly masters over everyday life, the awakening of remorse, and the reinforcement of inner contrasts in the society; since for other social groups just the opposite of the referred process became definitive, that is, the experience of recovering of history. In the wake of the upset of everyday life-worlds, the consequent political conflicts that seem to escalate and to endanger social normality, the increasingly unmanageable economic crisis, the total uncertainty and confusement towards all aspects of life is what has become a general and definitive experience, a dramatic cultural feeling following the collapse of socialism. The vision of post-modern philosophy and social theory about the end of "grands récits", the ceasing of the metadiscourses, the ensuing instability of social space, the loosening of familiar borders and accepted rules has become a historical experience here, in Eastern Europe, among the "ruins of socialism", on the threshold of mass pauperization and the total economic breakdown – and this fact has (and will have in the future) considerable consequences. The new owners of political power – supposedly uniformly all over Eastern and Southeastern Europe – in this situation consider past and the relation to past a (symbolic) tool, through which the uncertainty and confusion of social and political space can be diminished. Past certainly is not uniform, is not a homogeneous entity; past is of an uncertain expanse from the point of view not only of political systems, but of social strata and cultural worlds as well, it is a soft and flexible formation. That is why past is not reachable at hand every time and for everyone the same way; this past has to be created with the help of a retrospective mythology. The most significant phase in creating the past is the reestablishment of history as the only authentic point of reference for the present (cf. Elwert 1989: 441; Schiel 1985). However, history can be reestablished the time and the way historical or social memory (cf. Wachtel 1986; Halbwachs 1967) can be reconstructed. Nowadays there is nothing that would characterize Eastern and Southeastern Europe better, than this "reordering" of historical and/or social memory. But recalling past, rewriting history and reordering social memory are not at all "innocent" procedures; on the contrary, they involve serious consequences. One of the most significant consequences of these processes – at least from the point of view of nationalism – is the emergence of the category of collective identity (cf. Anthias 1992), the above mentioned cultural identity, and the "feeling of we" (cf. Kuzmics 1993) connecting closely to these identities.

There are two extremely deeply rooted forms of cultural identity today in Eastern and Southeastern Europe: the ethnic and the national identity. The most specific factor of the logic of these identities is the image of "we". The issue is, that this view can comprehend culture and cultural phenomena only in the terms of "our culture", and sees homogeneity, that is, sameness and uniformity as the most significant definitive quality of culture. The rewriting of the past, the colonization of history has not only political but cultural dimensions, as well, as it revives the historical concept of culture and identity from the 19th century, which has homogeneity as its main principle. The significance of the whole process in post-socialist countries is guaranteed such a way, that cultural identity, the "feeling of we" creates "the intimate feeling of protection" (cf. Finkielkraut 1990: 75), which is insured by a rediscovered authenticity and an obligatory homogeneity. *Cultural homogeneity*, created by symbolic instruments, the constancy, unchangedness of cultural identity rooting in it, the introduction of *past* into present through this constancy; *continuity*, as the guarantee of social, political and cultural legitimity, and, at the same time, as the tool of insuring cultural hegemony and political power – all together constitute a space in society and in history, which functions as a protected and a protecting zone where one can retire in unstable, confused historical and political situations. National culture and national identity have become categories serving to name this "safe site", although this safety is only imagined, as well as the pillars supporting these categories are imaginary. Post-socialism is a situation which is characterized by a confusion deriving from social and political problems, the unexpected freedom, and instability caused by these two factors. In this moment of social history those social movements, political ideas possessing "historical traditions" appear again, which place the return, the belonging to a linguistic and cultural community in the center of their ideology, as the single guarantee of social and cultural safety. Native language, the home-country, "ancient traditions" and norms fixed in them are again drawn in political usage, and are presented as instruments that are capable of ordering and stabilizing the world (cf. Hobsbawm 1991: 6). That this stability can be obtained only through the symbolic (and actual) exclusion of certain groups from the society, since this is the nature of its logic; that this logic necessarily – though certainly not always consciously – leads to xenophobia, murders and wars is denied by these movements and ideologies. Nevertheless, this denial does not alter the historical fact, that the struggle of the imagined "we" and the symbolic "they" results in real deaths; so that "we" could live, "they" have to be expelled or killed (cf. Gellner 1983: 2).

In Eastern and Southeastern Europe those forms and patterns of national identity are dominant today which were characteristic of the period between the two World Wars. These patterns of traditional national identity aim that "folk" as the standard conception of the political, social space should be filled up again with those conceptions, which had marked it in historical times preceding socialism. "Folk" in the context of modernity is a sociologically inarticulate and theoretically uninterpretable category; which becomes the main "subject" of belonging to a nation, the basis of collective solidarity due precisely to the fact, that by its inarticulateness, it goes beyond concrete social stratification and classification, cuts through the borders that separate social strata, and turns to be the symbol of that imaginary historical continuity, which is responsible for its birth (cf. Greenfeld 1990: 549–550; Estel 1991: 222). This understanding of folk and its representation on different stages of society is parallel with the earlier mentioned political, ideological effort to see nation as a cultural community or the desire to define it as a cultural community. Whenever nation is defined as a cultural community – as it is common in Eastern Europe, there is no need for the sociologically more specific description of the members of a nation and of the society; folk is a much more sufficient category for this aim.

At the same time, this unarticulated category of folk is closely connected to another element of national identity mentioned in the first part of this paper, which was present in the bud in the ideas of the 19th century. National ideologies strengthening after the breakdown of socialism made part of their argumentation the not particularly novel social-philosophical premiss, that is, people do not exist generally, humanity does not have a general cultural paradigm, there are only people, systems of value and life-worlds pertaining to particular nations.[4] Put it differently, the devotion to national culture, national traditions and national identity is not some manifestation of an ideology, rather the single possible mode of the social existence of man. It seems, that with the end of socialism, 19th century has returned to Eastern Europe. The struggle against universal self, global values, laws and norms has revived. In this struggle, the uniqueness of "popularism", the idea of "the spirit of the folk" gained a specific role (cf. Finkielkraut 1990: 17–19). Since socialism professed a kind of globality and universalism, therefore the new world following socialism could not follow a principle other than a special philosophy of "multiculturalism" based on national separateness and national differences. This specifically Eastern European version of multiculturalism follows a special logic. Outward, towards others, it insists on separation based on diversity, the importance of borders promoting the preservation of differences, and the independence and sovereignty of cultural worlds. But inward, in the direction of its own society it stresses the opposite of all. It demands uniformity and cultural homogeneity of the society, and does not endure cultural and social differences within the society, rather postulates inarticulateness – or, as national rhetoric puts it – unity, as the fundamental criteria of national existence. It is precisely this paradoxical logic that insures the efficacy of this system of thought. That is, on the one hand it claims that everyone has the right for cultural difference, moreover, that this is the basis of living in a society. However, on the other hand it demands that everyone should live among the similar; that there should be unambiguous borders between the dissimilar. This deformed concept of multiculturalism shows the mosaic-like order of separate, different, but inside ethnically and culturally "pure" worlds. The consequences of this philosophy are shown well by the current reality of the Eastern and Southeastern part of Europe.

Post-socialism and nationalism: a symbolic interpretation

One specific ideological foundation of resistance against socialism as a political system was the insistence upon national traditions, national identities, national rhetoric and national philosophy all over Eastern Europe. In the era of socialism national ideology and insistence upon national culture and identity appeared as such a unified worldview, which – in that particular social and political context – was capable of presenting itself as an actual political, social, and cultural alternative. However, as it obtained an authoritative, dominant position after the collapse of socialism, with the constant reference to national traditions and values, with their representation as models to be followed contributed not only to the revival of nationalism(s), but itself materialized as a nationalist ideology. This motive has to be emphasized: on the surface the social discourse is about national culture, traditions, identity, but this "language" in the depth – following from historical traditions necessarily, brings the idea, the ideology of nationalism into action. That is, it does not only mean that the "vacuum" left behind by socialism is filled up with nationalist ideologies, rather, that these ideas existed under the socialism as well imply different meanings in changing social and political context. The national ideology functioned under the socialism as an effective tool of political resistance turned after the breakdown of socialism into a powerful symbolical technique of political regime, of ideological domination.

The ideology of national leading to hidden nationalism, fulfills important functions in post-socialist societies, which is the result of at least two causes. On the one hand, post-socialist societies see world as something to be reconstructed. The world has to be reconstructed, because socialism was merely a historical cul-de-sac, that is, it does not constitute a part of (national) history, from which it has to be excluded; the world during the decades of socialism has gone so wrong, that it cannot be repaired further, this way the world has to be restituted – with the assistance of national ideology. However, on the other hand the change of Eastern European political systems means a transitory, a kind of *liminal* period burdened with symbolic dangers, in which the rules and laws of social structuring, social communication, and moving in social space become unstable, uncontoured, and obscure. The inside logic of the transitory situation and the feeling of threat deriving from it demands the same as the desire for the symbolic reconstruction of the world requires: that the unarticulated image of society, that is, nation, which can be described along one single parameter – along ethnicity or culture, suggesting symbolic equality, should be created and represented. Precisely in this particular social-historical moment of post-socialism appears or is revived the symbolic category of "Hungarian" ("Polish", "Slovak", "Romanian", etc.). These are not actually existing social roles or self-definitions, which convey actual cultural contents; rather, concepts created with the support of collective symbols and symbolic actions. The main function of these concepts is the introduction of a single – and dominant of all accidental criteria – structural factor, that is, "Hungarianness" (and imaginary national identity generally) in the transitory situation without explicit borders, roles and structures. "Hungarian" ("Polish", "Romanian", "Croatian", etc.) is a symbolic instrument, which in the liminal periods and crises of modern historical, social progress is capable of the creation of an unarticulated community. "Hungarian" – and national identity in this sense generally – serves as the ontology of the transitory situation as the primary tool of unarticulated orientation in the world. "Hungarian" is the symbolic concept, with the help of which social disintegration is abridgeable, this way an all-encompassing and all-pervasive "total", "whole" identity can be created. Through this instrument the individual will be linked to the imaginary community – not only in political, but in moral sense as well (cf. Finkielkraut 1990: 74, Estel 1991: 225). In the transitory situation this particular belonging to the imaginary community, the moral impact of this belonging is the motive of political action and the basis of the political field – and this particular element conveys the danger of the imaginary national identity. The dictatory of imaginary communities, the moral impact and force of national identities combined with the emotionalization and heroization of history, with the conscience of endangerment, with the conception of national history as subsequent tragedies, with the perpetual struggle against foreign enemies, and linked to the lack of rational intellectualism and critical traditions – these are the conditions of today's Eastern European political and social transition; the social-historical and cultural context of "Hungarian" as a symbolic concept. This symbolic concept has another important connotation as well. It is obvious nowadays, that in modern societies that are based on functional differentiation neither the ethnic, nor the national identity are able to fulfil the social functions of a well shaped social subsystem – the way like for example economy does. From this it follows, that nation cannot be seen other than a marker of identity, based on the consensus of adscriptive, collective values, which stands as an obstacle for the individual to get integrated into the increasingly compound social processes (cf. Nassehi 1990: 268–269). In other words, the question of "Hungarianness", of "What is Hungarian" is one striking symptom of anti-modernization, of counter-modernization for it only requires the identification with the above mentioned unarticulated community, and it does not demand from the individual the continual adaptation to changes expected by modern society; since "Hungarian" – and this interpretation of national identity generally – is a constant, everlasting, and unchanging factor of national existence.

At this point the usual interpretation of nationalism is broadened, and appears as a kind of worldview, which continuously reduces the diversity of the cultural context by establishing symbolic borders, outlining symbolic areas, integrating "the identical" and excluding "the others". This view strives to identify the world with small, apparent worlds, where clarity is guaranteed by sameness, uniformity, and homogeneity. The easier its borders are recognizable, the smaller the areas pressed between them, the less tolerance of "Otherness" needed; the safer the world (cf. Hobsbawm 1991: 199–200). For this particular reason the post-socialist version of nationalism is directed not only against other peoples and other cultures, but makes the awareness, understanding, interpretation, and acknowledgement of cultural otherness impossible within the society. Due to the myth of national culture, national identity, and the imaginary national community, cultural otherness in Eastern Europe equals to social and cultural marginality based on symbolic exclusion from the society, which manifests through this symbolic exclusion. Nationalism – in this interpretation – is not a "purely" historical or sociological category. Nationalism is rather to be seen as a "cultural system" (Kaschuba 1993: 269); as a special "style of thinking" (Greenfeld 1990: 549), as a kind of "knowledge postulated as a social property" (Estel 1991: 220), or as the "genre of collective imagination" (Spencer 1990: 285). There is a general social philosophy in Eastern Europe based on various thoughts like (a) struggle against globalization, (b) national uniqueness, (c) cultural homogeneity, (d) separation based on diversity, (e) preservation of differences against others, (f) a mosaic-like order of the world. This philosophy says, the only therapy against the infected world of socialism, and at the same time the only help in this dangerous situation of transition is the returning to the national roots, to the "natural" order of this world, to knit together ethnic and cultural homogeneity, moral order and symbolic purity. This approach and comprehension of the world represents a "new" cultural fundamentalism, and the new Eastern European nationalism is a striking manifestation of this fundamentalism. Cultural fundamentalism and the above mentioned Eastern European version of multiculturalism have a common philosophical background, "the idea of the bad outside and the good inside, the inside under attack and in need of protection" (Douglas 1970: 114). This is a philosophy, a worldview, an ideology based on "cathartic explanation" which means that social tensions, conflicts are "drained off by being displaced onto symbolic enemies". At the same time this is an ideology of "morale explanation" which means "the ability of an ideology to sustain individuals (or groups) in the face of chronic strains, either by denying it outright or by legitimizing it in terms of higher values" (Geertz 1973: 205). These theoretical statements turned into tragical reality on the Eastern European scene of political and social changes.

This cultural fundamentalism and "nationalism conveyed by culture" as a manifestation of it lives on as a "social myth" (cf. Barth 1959) profoundly impregnated in the everyday life of Eastern European societies, which manifests through prejudices, a false historical conscience, and ethnic stereotypes, and it becomes an unchallengeable and unverifiable experience originating from "the history". This social myth has been implicitly underlying the everyday life of Eastern European societies at least since the turn of the century and breaks to the surface in various historical eras with various intensity. When in history catastrophes and wars loom; when fundamental social and political changes initiate, when the pillars of social identity shake – at this moment this social myth flashes a vision of the future, the promise of a new and better world, the possibility of a mythic community. This myth lived its first real golden age after the First World War in Eastern Europe. At the time after the decline of the Austro-Hungarian Monarchy the "redistribution of the world" took place, when new social structures and political systems emerged. The second "golden age" is taking place in front of our eyes. This social myth is the sign and the symptom of a total political, philosophical, and ideological disorientation and confusion. It is an ideology, which attempts to find an answer and a cure for the confusion and the hopelessness stemming from it. It is a continual desperate effort to raise barricades against the modernizing world (cf. Hobsbawm 1991: 195). History, or the turmoil that is called so in Eastern Europe is unable to give a better device in this situation. Modernization that has never ended in Eastern Europe, the failure and the collapse of socialism lead to that "post-modern" that except the myth of cultural fundamentalism, of nationalism – it seems – cannot offer a different ideology.

This analysis may be gloomy, but is free from illusions. However, being free from illusions it points to the responsibility of social sciences and of the ethnographers or anthropologists. We can not alter the world but live in the conviction that it is possible and worth speaking and writing about it, and that this mode of writing can be acceptable epistemologically as well as morally. That is, we can contribute to the creation of a morally more acceptable world by speaking about it adequately. This is not much, but not little either; this is the duty of all of us.

Notes

An earlier version of this paper under the title "Ethnicity, Culture, and Nationalism" was presented on the meeting "Die Ethnisierung der Kultur" organized by the SIEF as a section of the 5th International Conference on Ethnographic Nationality Research in Békéscsaba, Hungary, 7–9 October 1993. I acknowledge with thanks for the helpful suggestions and comments made during the discussion by László Felföldi, Konrad Köstlin, and Anders Linde-Laursen.

1. I do not attempt here to review the whole litera-

ture concerning the concept of nation. As an example I refer only to the most recent summary of a broad perspective: Estel 1991.
2. I do not intend here to discuss the notion of folk culture. To the ethnographic discussion of this concept see Köstlin 1981, Köstlin 1984, Kaschuba 1988, Kaschuba 1990, Niedermüller 1991.
3. With a concern to this particular question significant researches have been effected first of all in Germany recently. Cf. Niethammer/von Plato/ Wierling 1991, Geiling-Maul and others 1992.
4. "There are no people generally in the world. I have only seen French, Italians, Russians in my life ... Concerning man in general sense, on the basis of my own experiences, I have to declare, that in case it does exist at all, it does so without me knowing about it." Joseph de Maistre: Œuvres complètes, I. Lyon, 1884. 75.

References

Anderson, B. 1983: *Imagined Communities. Reflections on the Origins and Spread of Nationalism.* London.

Anthias, F. 1992: Parameter kollektiver Identität: Ethnizität, Nationalismus, Rassismus. In: *Rassismus und Migration in Europe. Beiträge des Kongresses "Migration und Rassismus in Europa".* Hamburg, 1992: 88–103.

Assmann, A. 1991: Kultur als Lebenswelt und Monument. In: Aleida Assmann/Dietrich Harth (Hg.): *Kultur als Lebenswelt und Monument.* Frankfurt/M.: 11–25.

Barth, H. 1959: *Masse und Mythos. Die Theorie der Gewalt:* Georges Sorel. Reinbek, 1959.

Bauman, Z. 1990: Modernity and Ambivalence. In: Mike Featherstone (ed.): *Global Culture. Nationalism, Globalization and Modernity.* Theory, Culture & Society Special Issue. London: 143–170.

Bausinger, H. 1991: Volk und Sprache. Über eine mehrdeutige Beziehung. In: *Zeitschrift für Volkskunde,* 87: 169–180.

Clifford, J. 1983: On Ethnographic Authority. In: *Representations,* 1: 118–146.

Clifford, J. 1986: Introduction: Partial Truths. In: James Clifford/George E. Marcus (eds): *Writing Cultures. The Poetics and Politics of Ethnography.* Berkeley, 1986: 1–26.

Clifford, J. 1988: *The Predicament of Culture. Twentieth-Century Ethnography, Literature, and Art.* Cambridge.

Douglas, M. 1970: *Natural Symbols: Explorations in Cosmology.* New York.

Eisenstadt, S. 1991: Die Konstruktion nationaler Identitäten in vergleichender Perspektive. In: Bernhard Giesen (Hg.): *Nationale und kulturelle Identität. Studien zur Entwicklung des kollektiven Bewußtseins in der Neuzeit.* Frankfurt/M., 1991: 21–38.

Elwert, G. 1989: Nationalismus und Ethnizität. Über die Bildung von Wir-Gruppen. In: *Kölner Zeitschrift für Soziologie und Sozialpsychologie,* 41: 440–464.

Estel, B. 1991: Grundaspekte der Nation. Eine begrifflich-systematische Untersuchung. In: *Soziale Welt,* 42: 208–231.

Finkielkraut, A. 1990: *Die Niederlage des Denkens.* Hamburg.

Foster, R. 1991: Making National Cultures in the Global Ecumene. In: *Annual Review of Anthropology,* 20: 235–260.

Geertz, C. 1973: Ideology as a Cultural System. In: *The Interpretation of Cultures.* New York: 193–233.

Gellner, E. 1983: *Nation and Nationalism.* Ithaca-London.

Geiling-Maul, B./H. Macha/H. Schrutka-Rechtenstamm/A. Vechtel (Hg.) 1992: *Frauenalltag. Weibliche Lebenskultur in beiden Teilen Deutschlands.* Köln.

Giesen, B. 1991: Einleitung. In: Bernhard Giesen (Hg.): *Nationale und kulturelle Identität. Studien zur Entwicklung des kollektiven Bewußtseins in der Neuzeit.* Frankfurt/M., 1991: 9–18.

Greenfeld, L. 1990: The Formation of the Russian National Identity. The Role of Status Insecurity and Resentment. In: *Comparative Studies in Society and History,* 32: 549–591.

Halbwachs, M. 1967: *Das kollektive Gedächtnis.* Stuttgart.

Hobsbawm, E. 1991: *Nationen und Nationalismus. Mythos und Realität seit 1780.* Frankfurt/M.

Hofer, T. 1991: Construction of the "Folk Cultural Heritage" in Hungary. In: *Ethnologia Europaea,* 21: 145–170.

Kaschuba, W. 1988: Volkskultur zwischen feudaler und bürgerlicher Gesellschaft. Zur Geschichte eines Begriffs und seiner gesellschaftlichen Wirklichkeit. Frankfurt/M.

Kaschuba, W. 1990: Geschichte, Tradition, Alltagskultur. Zugangsweisen zum Begriff Volkskultur. In: Gertraud Krötz (Hg.): *Münchner Streitgespräche zur Volkskultur.* München: 22–27.

Kaschuba, W. 1993: Nationalismus und Ethnozentrismus. Zur kulturellen Ausgrenzung ethnischer Gruppen in (deutscher) Geschichte und Gegenwart. In: Michael Jeismann (Hg.): *Grenzfälle über neuen und alten Nationalismus.* Leipzig: 239–275.

Knorr-Cetina, K./Grathoff, R. 1988: Was ist und was soll kultursoziologische Forschung? In: Hans Georg Soeffner (Hg.): *Kultur und Alltagswelt.* Sonderband 6. Soziale Welt. Göttingen: 21–36.

Köstlin, K. 1981: Beschreibungsebenen der Volkskultur. In: *Kieler Blätter zur Volkskunde,* 13: 5–26.

Köstlin, K. 1984: Die Wiederkehr der Volkskultur. Der neue Umgang mit einem alten Begriff. In: *Ethnologia Europaea,* 14: 25–31.

Kuzmics, H. 1993: Einleitung. In: Reinhart Blomert u.a. (Hg.): *Transformationen des Wir-Gefühls. Studien zum nationalen Habitus.* Frankfurt: 7–41.

Lepsius, R. 1990: Nation und Nationalismus in

Deutschland. In: *Interessen, Ideen und Institutionen.* Opladen: 232–246.

Löfgren, O. 1989: The Nationalization of Culture. In: *Ethnologia Europaea,* 19: 5–23.

Marcus, G./Fischer, M. 1986: *Anthropology as Cultural Critique: An Experimental Moment in the Human Sciences.* Chicago.

Mommsen, H. 1987: Nation und Nationalismus in sozialgeschichtlicher Perspektive. In: Wolfgang Schieder/Volker Sellin (hg.): *Sozialgeschichte in Deutschland. Entwicklungen und Perspektiven im internationalen Zusammenhang.* Bd. II. Göttingen, 1987: 162–185.

Nassehi, A. 1990: Zum Funktionswandel von Ethnizität im Prozeß gesellschaftlicher Modernisierung. Ein Beitrag zur Theorie funktionaler Differenzierung. In: *Soziale Welt,* 41: 261–282.

Niedermüller, P. 1991: Die Volkskultur und die Symbolisierung der Gesellschaft: der Mythos der Nationalkultur in Mitteleuropa. In: *Tübinger Korrespondenzblatt* Nr. 40 (1991): 27–43.

Niethammer, L./A. von Plato/D. Wierling (Hg.) 1991: *Die volkseigene Erfahrung. Eine Archäologie in der Industrieprovinz der DDR.* Berlin.

Rupnik, J. 1990: Eisschrank oder Fegefeuer. Das Ende des Kommunismus und das Wiedererwachen der Nationalismen. In: *Transit,* 1: 132–141.

Schiel, T. 1985: Ethnie, Stamm, Nation – was ist Fiktion, was ist Realität? In: *Peripherie,* 18/19: 162–171.

Spencer, J. 1990: Writing Within. Anthropology, Nationalism, and Culture in Sri Lanka. In: *Current Anthropology,* 31: 283–300.

Steger, H. 1987: Deutsche Sprache und europäische Geschichte im östlichen Mitteleuropa. In: *Zeitschrift für Siebenbürgische Landeskunde,* 10: 129–161.

Wachtel, N. 1986: Memory and History: Introduction. In: *History and Anthropology,* 2: 207–224.

Weber, E. 1979: *Peasants into Frenchmen. The Modernization of Rural France, 1870–1914.* London.

Weber, M. 1922: *Wirtschaft und Gesellschaft.* Tübingen.

The Role of the International Exhibitions
in the Construction of National Cultures in the 19th Century

Bjarne Stoklund

> Stoklund, Bjarne 1994: The Role of the International Exhibitions in the Construction of National Cultures in the 19th Century. – Ethnologia Europaea 24: 35–44.
>
> In the latter half of the 19th century, the great international exhibitions, with their millions of visitors, grew into gigantic instruments for education and refinement where contemporary ideas were formulated and imprinted through visual communication, often in symbolic form (e.g. the aesthetic ideals of the bourgeoisie; human progress in evolutionary perspective; the superiority of the white race based on the sovereignty of the people). The article discusses the role played by the international exhibitions in the construction of what Orvar Löfgren has called an "international cultural grammar" of nationhood, choosing among other symbols the elements of folk culture that were later put on exhibition in the folk museums (folk costumes, vernacular buildings, peasant living rooms).
>
> *Professor Bjarne Stoklund, Institute of Archaeology and Ethnology, Vandkunsten 5, DK-1467 Copenhagen, Denmark.*

This article deals with one of the most crucial and fascinating cultural elements of the 19th century: *The great exhibitions.* I will argue that these exhibitions played an important part in the development of what Orvar Löfgren has called "an international cultural grammar of nationhood with a thesaurus of general ideas about the cultural ingredients needed to form a nation" (Löfgren 1989).

The exhibition is an innovation from the end of the 18th century and the beginning of the 19th century. It is related to phenomena such as the market and the trade fair, but it differs in the fact that exhibitions are not events for buying and selling, but only for presenting the latest products, tools and machines in order to stimulate "enterprise" and "progress".

In the latter part of the 19th century, this new phenomenon culminated in the institution which the French call *exposition universelle*, the English *international exhibition*, the Americans *world's fair*, and the Germans *Weltausstellung*. The idea was English; they arranged the first international exhibition in 1851, the so-called "Great Exhibition of the Works of Industry of All Nations", presented in Joseph Paxton's "Crystal Palace", a huge building of glass and iron, which heralded the development of a specific style of exhibition architecture. A few years later the French took over with the "exposition universelle" in Paris 1855, and although England arranged the next international exhibition in 1862, France remained on track as the leading exhibition nation for the rest of the century. All the French exhibitions were held in Paris: the second and most important in 1867, another one in 1878 in order to regain the position after the military defeat by Prussia, and again in 1889 in order to celebrate the centennial of the revolution, and finally in 1900 in order to mark the turn of the century. In between these were an Aus-

Fig. 1. The great exhibitions offered the organizers plenty of opportunities to stage national rituals. Here, the French president opens the 1878 Paris exhibition. – From *Illustreret Tidende* 1878.

trian "Weltausstellung" in 1873 and two American: in Philadelphia 1876 to celebrate the centennial of the declaration of independence, and in Chicago 1893, the so-called Columbian Exposition.[1]

In the last decades of the 19th century and in the beginning of the 20th, these international exhibitions were accompanied by a swarm of semi-international and national exhibitions. In the days when the "exhibition fever" culmi-

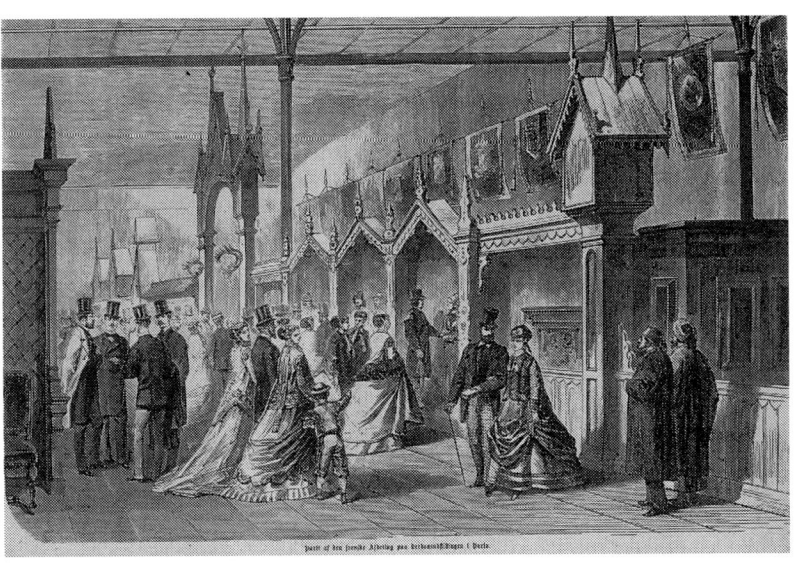

Fig. 2. The partition surrounding the Swedish section in Paris 1867 had been given a national touch inspired by the folk art, and it had been furnished with niches containing dummies in folk costumes.- From *Illustreret Tidende* 1867.

Fig. 3. A copy of the Ornäs-loft from Dalarna, one of the vernacular buildings, which were built in the park surrounding the main exhibition building at the 1867 Paris exhibition. The main exhibition building can be seen in the background. – From *Illustreret Tidende* 1867.

nated there was hardly a year without a major exhibition arrangement taking place in one or more of the larger cities of Europe.

The great exhibitions were by definition international, but from the very beginning they developed into a competition about the leading positions in industrial production between the industrialized nation states in Europe. In the words of Emperor Franz Joseph at the opening of the Vienna exhibition in 1873 it was "a peaceful international battle between all the civilized nations of the earth".

The American anthropologist Burton Benedict has compared the world's fairs to *potlaches*, the festivals of the Indian tribes of North West America, during which tribal chiefs established their position by ritual consumption and destruction of wealth (Benedict 1983). At the international exhibitions the competitors are not tribal chiefs, but nation states. However, in both cases there is a massive display of prestige in goods presented in a ritual manner. "Both potlaches and world's fairs tend to escalate," says Burton Benedict, "Each requires a bigger return prestation. To return an equal display would not increase the prestige of the giver. On the contrary, it would diminish it by showing that the giver was not able to exceed his rival. Every world's fair is trumpeted as being the biggest ever."

The 19th century exhibition organizers tried to exceed each other in the amount of exhibited goods, in the size of the exhibition area, in the amount of exhibition buildings , and, last but not least, in the number of visitors, which, by the way, reached impressive heights. The first international exhibition in 1851 was visited by almost 6 million; by 1900 the Paris exhibition reached a figure above 50 million visitors!

However, the competition was not just be-

Fig. 4. Siberian folk costumes at the Russian stand at the 1867 great exhibition. – From Ducuing 1867.

tween the organizers of the international exhibitions, but also between the exhibiting countries, who could read their relative placing in international evaluations, and in the amount of medals brought home as trophies from the exhibitions. It is a well-known fact that a feeling of decline in the aesthetic quality of Britain's technically superior industrial production, as it was presented at the Great Exhibition of 1851, gave the impetus to the founding of schools of arts and crafts, and to a museum of applied art in London, later to become the Victoria and Albert Museum. In a similar way, reports of the inferiority of Austrian industrial products at the London exhibition in 1862 paved the way for a founding of similar institutions in Vienna. And after the Paris exhibition in 1867, the history repeated itself, this time with Prussia, in the role of the defeated, deciding to improve the national products before the next international exhibition (Mundt 1974).

However, the international exhibitions do not merely try to exceed each other; to a large degree they also build on what the previous exhibitions have created. The rapid succession of international exhibitions in the latter half of the 19th century can be seen as a sort of relay race, in which the ideas and innovations introduced at one exhibition, are resumed and elaborated upon at the next one. In this way a set of rules of staging and a system of rituals are developed, which become regulars in the great exhibitions, not only the international, but also the geographically more delimited ones. In a similar way an exhibition language is gradually formed, in which ideas and norms can be passed on symbolically at the huge fora of visual communication, into which the international exhibition developed.

Due to the central position of the nation state in the overall exhibition landscape, it was important that a common non-verbal language was mastered, a visual code, in which the qualities of each nation, its specific style and its historic roots, could be expressed. Hereby the international exhibitions very actively came to bring about the selection of, and the elaboration of, the symbolic representations of the nations meeting at the great exhibitions.

From the very first international exhibitions, the different nations had their own sections in the large exhibition hall which held the whole exhibition. The sections were clearly marked with some of the standard symbols "through which an independent country proclaims its identity and sovereignty", as an oft quoted Indian pamphlet puts it (Löfgren 1989: 7–8): Name, coat of armour, and flag, the last two normally used to form a decorative whole.

From early on, the partitions between the national sections and the entrances to the sec-

Fig. 5. Thoroughbreds are paraded in front of the Russian building in Paris 1867. The roof ridge of the building is heavily decorated with symbolic details from vernacular architecture. – From *Illustreret Tidende* 1867.

tions were formed so that they not only were aesthetically pleasing, but also became the carriers of a national symbolism. There were two important sources to be drawn upon: Folk art and vernacular architecture or historic styles of specific national importance, for instance the "German renaissance" (cf. fig. 2).

However, the possibilities for a representation of the national culture were vastly extended, when the large central exhibition hall was complemented by national "pavilions", placed in the surrounding park. The first time it happened was in Paris 1867, and since then parks and pavilions have been a regular characteristic of the international exhibitions right up until the Expo 1992 in Seville. The pavilions were just one of the many important innovations of the 1867 exhibition whose chief organizer and man of ideas was the mining engineer and social scientist, Frederic Le Play. It was due to his initiative that general cultural and social themes became regular features at the world exhibitions. It can with some justification be said that from then on the international exhibitions were not only a competition in goods, but also in cultures.

One of his ideas was that the display of modern industrial production should be preceded by a historical thematic exhibition of "L'histoire du travail", showing human progress from the stone age to around 1800, thus giving an evolutionary perspective to the exhibition. However, this arrangement and similar ones at later exhibitions, also gave the young national museums of Europe an opportunity to display some of their archaeological treasures and thus to underline the deep historical roots of their national culture.

Not only archaeological but also ethnographical elements were added to the international exhibitions by the organizers of the 1867 Paris exhibition. In the classification system, drawn up by the imperial committee, there was a special class devoted to "costumes populaires des diverses contreés". At the exhibition there were costumes from most regions of France, and fifteen other countries had responded to the request of sending costumed figures to Paris (Collet 1987: 73). Dummies with folk costumes became a popular element at most of the subsequent international exhibitions; especially the Swedish groups, which were arranged in romantic folk life scenes, based on popular genre paintings, aroused the interest of the visitors (Berg 1980).

However, folk culture also made its entry into the park that surrounded the exhibition building in the 1867 exhibition. In this park it even more common today: A building designed by an architect symbolizing the country in question in a more sophisticated way.

But the idea of representations of vernacular architecture from all over Europe or the world, also caught on as a independent feature in the growing cultural or entertainment exhibition sector. This was typically buildings which not only had a local style, but which were also manned with representatives of the "local population". When, six years after the important Paris exposition, the Habsburg Monarchy was able to arrange its first international exhibition, the organizers had an ambi-

Fig. 6. At the modern international exhibitions, it is predominantly "third world" countries who use "ethnographic" or vernacular buildings as pavilions. Here is a part of the Arabian sector of the 1992 Seville exhibition. – Photo by B. Stoklund 1992.

was possible for the individual invited states to acquire a piece of land, where they could "display such objects as could serve to give a clear idea of the characteristics of the different peoples, such as their houses and their cuisines", to quote a Danish introduction to the exhibition. Not all states interpreted the request in the same way; the English, for instance, showed up with an electric lighthouse. But a large number of states, especially from Northern and Eastern Europe did display samples of national vernacular architecture. Rumania was represented by a small orthodox church, Norway displayed a splendid example of a loft-store from the Telemark landscape, and Russian craftsmen had built an *izba* with a stable. Austria was represented by a group of seven pavilions, each of them showing the local folk architecture of one of the provinces (cf. Stoklund 1993).

Several of these park pavilions were designed to accommodate an exhibition of national culture, and of national products. This idea was followed up at all of the subsequent international exhibitions: Here most countries designed their own national pavilions, more or less copying a national building – or, which is

Fig. 7. The Hungarian pavilion was one of the most symbolically charged at the 1992 Seville exhibition. Seven towers, which rose above the arched roof ridge, must be seen as a symbol of Transylvania (Siebenbürgen), today a part of Rumania. – From a leaflet about the Hungarian pavilion.

Fig. 8. The so-called "New England loghouse" at the exhibition in Philadelphia 1876, was inspired by "the ethnographical village" at the Vienna exhibition three years earlier. – From Leslie 1876.

tious plan for an "ethnographical village" which was supposed to include peasant houses from all over the world. Later on the plans were reduced to cover only the European countries, but even that proved to be impossible. The final result was a village at the Prater consisting of seven houses representing different provinces in Austria and Hungary, and two from the outside; one from Alsace and one from Russia (Pemsel 1989). At the later French and American international exhibitions, ethnographical elements like this were to play an even greater role. In Paris in 1889 one could visit a number of "native villages" peopled by some five hundred natives from Africa, Asia, and America, and at the Chicago World's Columbian Exposition in 1893 one could visit a Bedouin camp, a Red Indian Village, a Lapp camp, a Persian palace, a Chinese market, a Japanese bazaar, and villages from Samoa, Java, and Dahomey. European folk culture was represented by villages from Germany, Austria, Ireland, and other countries (Bancroft 1893).

Costumes and buildings were two folk cultural features of the international exhibitions. Living rooms were a third element; they could easily be fitted into an exhibition hall and they could, when richly equipped with furniture and "peopled" with dummies in local costumes, present a full image of a folk culture. At the same time, they emphasized the homely cosiness and the cheerful contentment which always lies as an undercurrent in the presentation of folk culture at the international exhibitions.

The living room from Hindelopen in West Friesland, presented by the Dutch organizers at the 1878 Paris exhibition, became especially popular. It had an exceptionally strong effect because it was arranged in such a way that it not only was possible to look into the living room, but also to step into it, which gave a strong personal feeling of visiting a past world. The Hindelopen living room inspired the Danish museum founder Bernhard Olsen to try something similar, at a Danish exhibition the following year, with a living room from the island of Amager near Copenhagen (de Jong & Skougaard 1993).

Neither the Friesian living room from Hindelopen nor the Amager living room, which, in fact, represented the culture of former immigrants from the Netherlands, can be said to be typical representatives of respectively the Dutch and the Danish national culture. Nonetheless they both came to function as national symbols. This example touches upon a characteristic feature of the selection process, which takes place at the international exhibitions in this field. It is not the most characteristic national cultural elements which find the favour

Fig. 9. Living room from Amager near Copenhagen with dummies in folk costumes, arranged by Bernhard Olsen at an exhibition in Copenhagen 1879. – From Nyrop 1879.

of the eyes of the organizers, but rather the peculiar, the picturesque, the exotic. Here, as in other fields, the *potlach* effect makes itself manifest, it is a competition in culture: What is important is to exceed each other. And in this way the great exhibitions also contribute to single out "the specifically national areas", which certainly are not always too apparent: Dalarna in Sweden, Telemarken in Norway, Tirol in Austria, or the Pusztas of the great Hungarian Plain.

The Friesians, situated by the North Sea on Dutch and German territories and bordering up to Denmark, suffered the fate of having their ethnic culture turned into something "Old-Dutch" in the Netherlands, something seen as particularly and genuinely Germanic in Germany, and something used as an inspiration for the recreation of a "Danish Classicism" in the countryside of Denmark (cf. Stoklund 1990). The Hindelopen living rooms became a coveted collector's item in Germany, where at least Rudolph Virchow's museum in Berlin and the "Germanisches Museum" in Nürnberg acquired examples of this "Proto-Germanic" room (de Jong & Skougaard 1993).

In this context it may be justified to mention another of the great founders of museums: Heinrich Sauermann in Flensburg, who created the northernmost German museum of applied art and folk culture (Redlefsen 1976).

Sauermann was a cabinet maker by profession, and he took part in the development of a specific German national renaissance style within the area of interior design. He took his inspiration from living rooms in the North Friesian islands which he exhibited in his museum. With magnificent renaissance rooms designed with Friesian inspiration, he visited several of the great exhibitions, amongst others the international exhibitions in Chicago 1893 and in Paris 1900. In the beginning he called the room on display "Nordfriesisches Zimmer", but characteristically he later renamed it "Niederdeutsches Zimmer", in that way changing ethnic style into national culture.

The development of folk and open-air museums in several European countries at the end of the 19th century can be seen as a sort of permanent-making of sectors of the great exhibitions: The essential parts of the new museum concept had been shaped by the exhibition organizers, who also had selected what was to become the most important features of these museums: Folk costumes, representatives of vernacular architecture, peasant living rooms, and the decorated domestic utensils, which came to be known as "folk art" at the turn of the century (cf. Stoklund 1993).

But the role of the great exhibitions may have had an even further reaching influence in

Fig. 10. Viking motives became popular among Scandinavian participants in the great exhibitions in the 1870s, used e.g. on silver ware. Here a viking ship advertises a Norwegian ironworks, an early example of a still well-known phenomenon. – From Leslie 1876.

this field. It is a well known fact that the emphasis of the scientific exploration of the folk culture, in the first half of the 19th century, lay on the spiritual or folkloristic elements: folk ballads, fairy tales, popular beliefs, etc. But in the last half of the century an essential part of the scholarly interest turned towards "material" culture, with costumes and buildings as the preferred subjects of study. It is hardly possible to imagine that this shift of emphasis could have taken place without the international exhibitions and their demand for material cultural elements for a visual communication of the national cultures of Europe.

It is easy to give several concrete examples, which show that the exhibitions not only have inspired the establishment of museums, but also triggered research projects within this field.

Let me try to summarize. In the latter half of the 19th century, the development of an industrial culture and the establishment of nation states were closely connected processes. The technological and social development was pushed forward by the competition among the nation states, who pitted themselves against each other and sized each other up at the great exhibitions. Their common project was progress and modernization; their object was to learn the most from each other in the quickest possible way through the communication of news, which, amongst others, the exhibitions represented. For the individual nation state the object was to be in the front line of the modernization. But at the same time as the states proved their modernity and competitive power, it was important to stress what separated the individual state from the others: the national culture. Two aspects of the material culture came to play a special part: Prehistoric finds, demonstrating the deep historical origins of the nation state, and the so-called "folk culture", representing the genuine, national character. Historical venerableness and distinctive national characteristics were values which easily let themselves be mediated through the visual communication, within the framework of the exhibition.

But, hereby, the role of these features of the exhibition are not exhausted. In the national project, modernity and conservatism walk hand in hand, they are complementary traits in a quite paradoxical manner. Confronted with continually new examples of the Titanesque technical advance, the visitors needed to be reassured that something was permanent, that the country and the people possessed an unyielding constancy, and that the bourgeois values, mostly tied to the home and the family, would be continued in spite of the upheavals. That was the message which the peasant living rooms and the folk costumes, amongst others, passed on to the exhibition visitors.

Note

1. Of the extensive recent literature on the international exhibitions in the 19th century we may mention Luckhurst 1951, Allwood 1977, Findling 1990 and Benedict 1983. Rydell 1985 deals with the American exhibitions 1876–1916 and Pemsel 1989 with the Austrian exhibition 1873. Mogensen 1993 surveys the Danish participation in the international expositions 1851–1900. In a recent publication (Ehn et al. 1993) Orvar Löfgren has given examples of how Scandinavian national culture was presented at the great exhibitions.

References

Allwood, John 1977: *The Great Exhibitions*. London.
Bancroft, H.H. 1893: *The Book of the Fair. An Historical and Descriptive Presentation of the World's Science, Art and Industry, as viewed through the Columbian Exposition at Chicago in 1893.* Chicago/San Francisco.
Bauer, Ingolf 1991: Bürgerzimmer und Bauernstuben im Museum. In: *Möbel aus Franken. Oberflächen und Hintergründe. Ausstellungskatalog,* München.
Benedict, Burton 1983: *The Anthropology of World's Fairs.* London/Berkeley.
Berg, Jonas 1980: Dräktdockor – Hazelius och andras. In: *Fataburen.*
Collet, Isabelle 1987: Les premiers musées d'ethnographie régionale en France. In: *Muséologie et ethnologie.* Paris.
de Jong, A. A. M. & Mette Skougaard 1993: The Hindelopen and the Amager Rooms: Two examples of an historical museum phenomenon. In: *Journal of the History of Collections* 5 no. 2.
Ducuing, M. Fr. (ed.) 1867: *L'exposition universelle de 1867 I–II.* Paris.
Ehn, Billy, Jonas Frykman, and Orvar Löfgren 1993: *Försvenskningen av Sverige. Det nationellas förvandlingar.* Stockholm.
Findling, John E. (ed.) 1990: *Historical Dictionary of World's Fairs and Expositions, 1851–1988.* New York/London.
Leslie, Frank (ed.) 1876: *Illustrated Historical Register of the Centennial Exposition 1876.* Philadelphia, repr. New York 1976.
Luckhurst, K.N. 1951: *The Story of Exhibitions.* London/New York.
Löfgren 1989: The Nationalization of Culture. In: *Ethnologia Europaea* XIX.
Mogensen, Margit 1993: *Eventyrets tid. Danmarks deltagelse i verdensudstillingerne 1851–1900.* Landbohistorisk Selskab.
Mundt, Barbara 1974: *Die deutschen Kunstgewerbemuseen im 19 Jahrh.* München.
Nyrop, C. 1879: *Fra den kunstindustrielle Udstilling.* Copenhagen.
Pemsel, Jutta 1989: *Die Wiener Weltausstellung. Das gründerzeitliche Wien am Wendepunkt.* Wien/Köln.
Redlefsen, Ellen 1976: Heinrich Sauermann – ein Möbelfabrikant und Museumsgründer vor 100 Jahren. In: *Nordelbingen* 45.
Rydell, Robert W. 1984: *All the World's a Fair. Visions of Empire at American Expositions, 1876–1916.* Chicago/London.
Stoklund, Bjarne 1990: Stiftung von Erinnerung im Wandel musealer Konzepte. In: *Erinnern und Vergessen. Vorträge des 27. Deutschen Volkskundekongresses 1989. Beiträge zur Volkskunde in Niedersachsen* 5.
Stoklund, Bjarne 1993: International Exhibitions and the New Museum Concept in the Latter Half of the Nineteenth Century. In: *Ethnologia Scandinavica* vol. 23.

Putting a Mirror to People's Lives
Cultural Brokerage, Folklore, and Multiculturalism

Gisela Welz

> Welz, Gisela 1994: Putting a Mirror to People's Lives. Cultural Brokerage, Folklore, and Multiculturalism. – Ethnologia Europaea 24: 45–49.
>
> In the United States, folklorists are entering the public sector. With the advent of multicultural programs in education and cultural politics, so-called public folklorists are increasingly assuming a new role in cultural brokerage, mediating the relationship between immigrant cultures and the wider public. This paper contends that rather than reflecting cultures "as in a mirror", public folklore entails representational practices that invent cultural otherness.
>
> *Gisela Welz, Hochschulassistentin, Ludwig-Uhland-Institut für Empirische Kulturwissenschaft, Universität Tübingen, Schloß, D-72070 Tübingen, Germany*

Today, immigration is making postindustrial Western societies more culturally diverse than ever. Big cities are emerging as culturally vibrant, but socially polarized catalysts of globalization. In global cities,[1] immigrant cultures and the immigration experience itself have become topics of cultural politics and commodities in cultural markets. In New York City, for instance, a plethora of cultural institutions function as showcases for the folk cultures of ethnic minorities who have made this city their new home. Since the mid-eighties, there has been a marked increase in the number of not-for-profit organizations in New York City who support the cultural practices of immigrants. They attempt to bring immigrants' cultural creativity to public attention, and try to preserve cultural establishments and landmarks of immigrant cultures. They do so by creating exhibits, by organizing performances and concerts, by working closely with masters of traditional arts, by creating archives and documentations, videos and radio broadcasts, festivals and parades.

Many of the experts working in these institutions have received academic training as folklorists. They call themselves public sector folklorists, in order to contrast their endeavours with those of academic folklore. In the political framework of multiculturalism, American folklorists succeed in carving out professional roles for themselves. They are making foreign cultural expressions accessible to American audiences and, in urban cultural politics, are closing the cultural gap between newcomers and those residents of the city who have been here a while. In cooperation with anthropologists, ethnomusicologists and social historians also working in this field, folklorists act as cultural brokers mediating the relationship between immigrant cultures and a wider cultural market.

In 1992 und 1993, I conducted fieldwork among public sector folklorists – "public folklorists" for short – in New York City. My ethnography of ethnographers focussed on projects and programs that represent the cultures of immigrants as well as the culture of immigration.[2] In New York, the institutional landscape of promoting cultural diversity ranges from large institutions of national importance like the *Ellis Island Immigration Museum* to small localized establishments like the *Lower East Side Tenement Museum*. On Ellis Island, a former government facility for the processing of immigrants has been transformed into a multimillion dollar exhibition, located in the original rooms where the new arrivals were subjected to scrutiny by immigration officers. The *Lower East Side Tene-*

ment Museum is rebuilding a turn-of-the-century immigrants' dwelling, aiming to fill it with museum pieces as well as with trained actors who will replicate the everyday life of past immigrant populations. Other institutions, such as the *World Music Institute* or the *Ethnic Folk Arts Center*, have specialized in featuring immigrant music and dance. A prominent institution called *City Lore* – The New York Center for Urban Folk Culture – is committed to presenting and preserving the "living heritage" and the diversity of New York neighborhood and community life: "Just as this city is one of the so-called 'high culture' centers of the world, so it is one of the richest and most diverse centers of traditional folk culture – New York City may well boast the most diverse aggregate of ethnic groups in the world. This diversity is a source of both cultural wealth and cultural conflict; *City Lore* draws on the folk culture of the city to tap this wealth and to help ease the conflicts that so often develop out of cultural ignorance" (Pearson 1992, 1). *City Lore* is pursuing this goal by various activities in the fields of presentation – festivals, exhibitions, radio broadcasts –, interpretation – films and art projects –, documentation, and education. Products of City Lore's work range from a book on children's games on city streets to an exhibition of ethnic social clubs in New York, immigrant voluntary associations that often meet in disused stores on street level for lack of other meeting places.

Most of these projects and institutions probably would not exist without public grants from the *Folk Arts Program* of the *New York State Council on the Arts*. The *Council on the Arts*, New York State's agency for funding the arts and cultural programs all over the state, has folk arts as a special funding category side by side with more established categories as classical music and ballet. This is a result of folklorists' lobbying political support for the preservation of traditional, folk and minority cultures. It also speaks to the growing attention and financial support for cultural conservation on the national level in the United States, such as evidenced in the creation of a Folk Arts Program in the National Endowment for the Arts in 1974. All of these developments – the growth of public institutions that showcase folk cultural expressions, the inclusion of folk arts in the state funding for cultural programs, and the increasing professionalization of folklorists who work outside the traditional fields of academic folklore – reflect the emergence of public folklore as an autonomous branch of folklore practice that is considered equal to the university-based folklore scholarship. In the eighties and nineties, folklore in the public sector is superceding the antagonism of pure versus applied folklore by taking up again where New Deal folklore programs and the Federal Writers' Project had left off (Hirsch 1988).

American public folklore in many ways does not differ much from its European counterparts, both contemporary and historical. Not only as an applied science, but just the same within the academy, folklore has always been a discipline of an essentially applied character, acting as a mediator of "tensions between national identity and state building" (Kirshenblatt-Gimblett 1988:143). Specific to public folklore in America, however, is its emphasis on cultural pluralism. Public folklore is committed to maintaining cultural diversity, defending it against homogenizing influences of any kind. Roger Abrahams has pointed out that at the inception of folklore as a discipline in the United States, "the relation between indigenous vernacular language and lore, on the one hand, and the nation-state, on the other, was far from fully established" (Abrahams 1992:250), contrary to the situation in Europe. In this tradition,[3] public folklore today perceives as its obligation the facilitation of cultural dialogues between recent arrivals in American society and the more established segments of the population. It aims to make visible the traditions of immigrants and ethnic minorities and to create appreciation and understanding for cultural differences within American society. It is of course no coincidence that public folklore comes to prominence at a time when multiculturalism is being promoted in American society. Barbara Kirshenblatt-Gimblett critically noted in her presidential address at the 1992 American Folklore Society meeting that folklorists are in the business of producing multiculturalism.[4] Folklorists do not merely profit from the new political support for multicultural programs, but are actively involved in constructing and inventing cultural otherness.

When I asked one of the practitioners in New York's "multiculturalism business" about her interpretation of the role of public folklorists in society, she said, "Putting a mirror to people's lives, and saying: what you are doing is important, is of cultural value". Her response was fairly typical; I encountered similar descriptions of folklorists' practice in many of my interviews with museums curators, ethnographers, grant makers, exhibit designers, photographers, and artists involved in the folklorist enterprise. What public sector folklorists do – according to their self-image – is that they validate other people's everyday lives as valuable cultural expressions. By "mirroring", folklorists transform the patterns and rhythms of these lives into something that can be looked at and listened to in the much larger arenas of education and entertainment – that is, in a concert hall, in a museum, on the movie screen or on television.

"Putting a mirror to people's lives" is a widespread, but highly questionnable conceptualization of the kind of representational work that folklorists are doing when they create exhibitions, write monographs, present folk musicians on stage, or assemble archival documentations. The metaphor of "mirroring" hides several problematic issues in folklorists's practice. These I intend to make visible by asking – and answering – a series of questions.

First: Who is holding the mirror? Usually the folklorist is. The separation between who is mirrored and who has the privilege of holding the mirror is increasingly surmounted by minority scholars and artists who themselves take charge of cultural productions. In most cases, however, it is still a matter of advocacy rather than of self-representation of cultural groups, that is, of operating from a position outside rather than inside the cultural context that is being represented. Folklorists in the public sector often claim to occupy a unique in-between-position, belonging neither to the cultural groups they present nor to the audience, but imagining themselves to be a link, a bridge between the two.

Second: How does the mirror image come about? The notion of representation that employs the metaphor of the mirror is more than just simplistic. It is wrong. Folklore does not function as a mirror that merely replicates and never distorts. Even though the folklorist stays invisible behind the mirror, he or she nevertheless takes an active role in constructing the images of cultural otherness it presents. Images resulting from representational work are never unmediated. Also one has to take into consideration that whenever public folklorists showcase cultural traditions, they do so by operating within the confines of specific genres of representing culture, such as museum exhibits, on-stage performance presentations, documentary films, or guided tours. As recent work in critical anthropology and ethnographic writing has shown, power and history work through such cultural productions in ways their authors or producers cannot fully control (Clifford 1986:7).

Third: What does the mirror show? Obviously, the mirror does not show everything. It is always angled as to reflect certain things and to deflect others. What the folkloric mirror shows the spectator's gaze is the "traditional", the "authentic", and the culturally "pure". Conventional paradigms of folk culture, community, and ethnicity prevail in public folklore practice. Among public folklorists, the term *community*, infusing that bounded cultural grouping with notions of belongingness and identity, largely is taken as a given not requiring explanation or inquiry. The funding guidelines of folk arts grant makers speak of a sharedness of the way of life that produces traditional cultural expressions maintained and passed on by a group – whose boundedness and homogeneity remains largely unquestionned. Contemporary findings of critical folklore and anthropology that point to a heterogeneity of cultural experience within groups claim that cultural identities are processual rather than stable, emergent rather than fixed. These do not find recognition in public folklore. The notion of the sharedness of culture remains a guiding principle for much of the cultural work representing immigrant culture, and public folklorists remain to be most concerned with salvaging "authentic" expressions of immigrant or minority cultures while ignoring what they consider "inauthentic". As a consequence, many immigrant artists criticize Public Folklore's disregard of the ongoing processuality of culture in their communities. One immigrant musician I encountered in the course of my fieldwork plays a traditional instrument and sings in his native language. His productions, however, are neither traditional enough for public folklore funding nor commercial enough for market-oriented recording companies and promoters. He angrily attacked what he felt is a "colonial attitude" that tries to hold his group's culture in a position of fixedness in time and space, denying development and change. This brings us to our final question.

Fourth: Why are public folklorists today putting their disciplinary "mirrors" to immigrants' lives? The majority of public folklore projects and programs in New York are engaged in sophisticated folklorizations of immigrants' cultural practices. The expressions they select for preservation and presentation are usually aesthetically pleasing, academically challenging, and also sufficiently foreign to provide an exotic thrill. Music and dance are selected for their vibrancy and expressiveness; bits and pieces of everyday lives are shown for their apparent modesty, simplicity, and authenticity, contrasting nicely with the everyday lives of average Americans in the 1990s.

The work of many public folklorists indeed seems driven by a feeling that recent transformations of American society are threatening people's well-being. One of the folklorists interviewed in the course of my research claimed that "what we do as public folklorists is a reaction against postmodernity". He and his colleagues perceive that recent processes of social change are cutting people from their roots, fragmenting their lives, and severing their connections to stable contexts such as communities. Nevertheless, "people still want to feel rooted and connected and interpersonal". And this is where the cultural productions of public folklore come in to tell people that rootedness is still possible, even though endangered, and that certain segments of society, especially immigrant groups, are pockets of rootedness, connectedness, and intact interpersonal relations. One impetus for preserving and presenting immigrant and ethnic cultures, then, seems to be the desire of mainstream America for regaining authenticity and immediacy in its social relations, a desire that is fueled by and gains in urgency along with the postmodern transformations of society.

By emphasizing what is colorful, vibrant and refreshingly simple about immigrant cultures, public folklore is feeding into what anthropologist Fred Myers[5] recently has called "the difference machine", the process of commodifying the exotic, the culturally other for consumption. Obviously, a deep ambivalence arises out of trying to stem the tide of postmodernity by holding on to the very modern paradigm of cultural loss and folkloric rescue. By attempting to stave off postmodernity, public folklore is becoming a functional and functioning element of the postmodern process, a handmaiden to its very commodification of culture and to the appropriation and colonization of the vernacular that is so characteristic of the contemporary politics of culture.

In conclusion, however, I would predict that public folklore will find it increasingly difficult to project its notions of culture, tradition, and identity onto the everyday life practices and discourses of minorities in a city like New York. For one, traditionality seems to acquire a different meaning under conditions of postmodernity that even those who operate with older paradigms cannot fully escape. Today, traditionality's referent is no longer continuity, but instead, rupture and discontinuity. The people who are represented as "folk" are not among the last to acknowledge that. Casitas – "little houses" – are a type of Puerto Rican handmade vernacular architecture constructed on empty lots in New York City's *latino* neighborhoods. Usually, a group of men will get together to form a casita club, to build a small wooden house and to lay out a small garden. The casita serves as a meeting place after work and on weekends; "traditional" music and "traditional" food are foci of sociability.

Casitas are a good example for the process in which marginal urban populations actively use traditionality as a competitive resource. As the president of one casita club in New York's South Bronx explained to me in an interview, his casita club's efforts at upholding "tradition" in the Bronx are primarily a response to the living conditions in their drug-infested low income neighborhood of the South Bronx. Their decision to build a casita some years ago was a strategic choice that has more to do with where and how they live in New York than with continuing a tradition they imported from Puerto Rico. City government and political elites are generally supportive of groups that uphold traditional values like "family" and "community"; the casita club attempts to bank on that support. With the casita people, "tradition" is but one possible trope of cultural strategizing. Under different conditions, they may have opted for "modernization" instead. The identity this type of cultural strategizing generates is optional: It is not even for everyone who is Puerto Rican and lives in the South Bronx. The identity of being a casita club member is also provisional: there is no telling for how long it will offer stability, both to the group and to the individual. Tradition is no longer a place that any of these men who have built a casita together can go back to. But not merely because in Puerto Rico, casita building is a thing of the past. Rather, as James Clifford is claiming, "there is no going back, no essence to redeem" (Clifford 1988:4).

References

Abrahams, Roger D. 1992: "The Foundations of American Public Folklore". In: Robert Baron and Nicholas R. Spitzer (eds): *Public Folklore*, Washington/London: 245–261.
Clifford, James 1986: "Partial Truths". In: George E. Marcus and James Clifford (eds): *Writing Culture. The Poetics and Politics of Ethnography*, Berkeley: 1–26.
Clifford, James 1988: "Introduction: The Pure Products Go Crazy". In: James Clifford: *The Predicament of Culture. Twentieth-Century Ethnography, Literature, and Art*, Cambridge, Mass./London: 1–17.
Hannerz, Ulf 1993: "The Cultural Role of World Cities". In: Anthony P. Cohen and Katsuyoshi Fukui (eds): *Humanising the City? Social Contexts of Urban Life at the Turn of the Millennium*, Edinburgh: 69–83.
Hirsch, Jerrold 1988: "Cultural Pluralism and Applied Folklore. The New Deal Precedent". In: Burt Feintuch (ed.): *The Conservation of Culture. Folklorists and the Public Sector*, Lexington, Kentucky: 46–67.
Kirshenblatt-Gimblett, Barbara 1988: "Mistaken Dichotomies". In: *Journal of American Folklore*, 101 (400): 140–155.
Pearson, Nathan W., Jr. 1992: "From the President". In: *City Lore. Documenting, preserving and presenting New York's folk culture*, New York: 1.
Sassen, Saskia 1991: *The Global City*. New York, London, Tokyo. Princeton.

Notes

1. The term "global city" was coined by economists and sociologists to denote major cities that take a leading role in global economic and social transformations (see Sassen 1991). Ulf Hannerz has introduced the term "world city" into anthropological discourse, applying it to cities that function as catalysts in global cultural processes (see Hannerz 1993).
2. From October 1992 to March 1993, I was affiliated as a visiting scholar to the Department of Performance Studies, New York University, New York. My research was funded by the American Council of Learned Societies in its American Studies Fellowship Program.
3. Among historians of folklore scholarship, there is an ongoing dispute about whether public folklore shares the same romanticist roots as nationalism – suggested by folklorists' endorsement of such motifs as "discovering the common experience of becoming an American" – or whether, to the contrary, public folklore's promoting an awareness of diversity within American society may stem nationalist impulses (Hirsch 1988; Abrahams 1992).
4. Barbara Kirshenblatt-Gimblett's Keynote Address at the 1992 American Folklore Society's Annual Meeting in Jacksonville, Florida, was titled "Bones of Contention, Bodies of Knowledge: Folklore's Crisis".
5. In a lecture in Prof. Barbara Kirshenblatt-Gimblett's seminar "Tourist Productions", Department for Performance Studies, New York University, on February 25, 1993.

Ethnic Consciousness and Cohabitation
in a Slovak-Hungarian Village Community

Zita Škovierová

Škovierová, Zita 1994: Ethnic Consciousness and Cohabitation in a Slovak-Hungarian Village Community – Ethnologia Europaea 24: 51–58.

The article is a microsonde into the social relations of a Slovak-Hungarian village community. Determinants influencing the 20th century ethnic consciousness and cohabitation of ethnically mixed region in southern Slovakia are being analyzed. The changes of ethnicity and mutual relationship of Slovaks and Hungarians were mostly influenced by extralocal factors (historical events, political changes, influence of surroundings). Intralocal factors (family, kinship and other informal groups) were consolidating the cohabitation of its population. In traditional community ethnic influences intermingled with religious ones. Village authorities and ambitions of individual people played an important role, too.

Zita Škovierová, PhD, research fellow, Department of Ethnology, Comenius University, 818 01 Bratislava, Slovakia.

Imeû, a village in the Danube lowlands, is situated 20 km northwards of the Slovak–Hungarian state border (Komarno district). Inhabitants of this area were well up to the 20th century the bearers of middle European culture of the so-called Panonian type. After Turkish invasions the devastated land was colonized by Slovaks who proceeded to develop peasant culture. Due to strong Hungarianization since the late 19th century a great majority of local Slovaks were Hungarianized. More Slovaks were coming from northern areas and settled there. Cultivation of corn, root-crops, vine, cattle and sheep breeding were the main subsistence sources in the first half of this century. In their region Imeû inhabitants excelled in cultivation of tobacco, vegetables and in domestic craft. After agricultural collectivization which ended in 1959, a minority of the inhabitants were involved in farming, while the majority of them worked in industry or in the sphere of services in nearby towns. Since the 1970's cultivation of vegetables is an additional job of all families and a favourable source of higher family incomes.

Finding this locality for my research was more incidental than deliberate. I was attracted by the village which is claimed Slovak and yet my colleagues who did not speak Hungarian had problems to communicate with its inhabitants in Slovak when carrying out their research. The second curiosity was the cancellation of Hungarian school and maintenance of Slovak school. I wanted to find out what caused this paradox between the attitudes and behaviour of Imeû inhabitants.

I followed the factors influencing the ethnic consciousness and declaration of ethnicity of its inhabitants and their cohabitation. They may be divided into extralocal (external) and intralocal (internal) factors. The former comprise historical events, political changes and measures on a general level which happened without direct action of local community members (sometimes even against their will). Objectively existing phenomena of wider (regional) application belong there too. The latter group of factors includes undertakings of formal institutions on the local level (state administration, educational system, church) and also undertakings of informal, small social groups. I also enclose here factors connected

Fig. 1. Traditional type of village clay house with a thatched roof. Photo: Slovak Institute for Monuments' Preservation 1960.

with the individual personality, his social status and character.

Significant break-through events which principally influenced ethnic consciousness and life in ethnically mixed localities were historical events and political measures. Disintegration of multinational Austro-Hungarian Monarchy was the first historical turning point. In 1918 the Czechoslovak republic was formed. The Trianon treaty divided the territory of Hungary and Czechoslovakia at the Danube river. Annexation of this part of Czechoslovak territory by Hungary during Horthy's occupation in 1938–1945 was next interference. After World War II the exchange of some Hungarians from southern Slovakia with Slovaks from Hungary in 1946–47 followed and the so-called re-Slovakization action "the return of re-Magyarized people in Slovakia to the Slovak nation" (Šutaj, 1992: 182).

Ethnical and cultural influence of inhabitants from surrounding villages also formed ethnocultural orientation of Imeû inhabitants. In the past Imeû was one of the villages which mostly interferred with an area where the population spoke Hungarian. Neighbouring villages as well as wider environment were prevailingly inhabited by a population of Hungarian nationality. Hungarian as the main communicative language provided greater possibilities of mutual contacts. Through mixed marriages this influence was transferred into the investigated village. Work contacts and visits of cultural events in surrounding villages had a similar effect.

In Imeû the forms of job migration were already highly developed in the first half of the 20th century. Especially landless people and small farmers who had no means of subsistence took advantage of migration for job. They migrated particularly to estates where they carried out mostly agricultural, gardening and seasonal work. There they generally met Hungarian speaking population. Less often they were able to meet Slovak workers from northern regions who lived and worked there in summer. After-war and prolonged job migration to more distant Slovak or Czech enterprises did not seriously affect the migrants – coming home they again spoke Hungarian as it

Fig. 2. Family cooperative ties are very firm in Imeû: Women of three generations clean and prepare home bred poultry for storing (1993).

was more in use in the village. At present the majority of inhabitants work in the nearest surroundings and due to economic recession they have increased cultivation of vegetables – they stay under the influence of local environment.

Local administration was subordinate to village nationality and ruling political regime. Accordingly the village was alternately pro-Hungarian and pro-Czechoslovak and it was governed by issued laws and regulations in contact with inhabitants, depending on the characters and ambitions of local cancellors and to what extent they followed the laws and regulations which contradicted the interests and needs of the local public.

There were two church communities in Imeû: Roman Catholics and Calvinists. In 1930 1 777 inhabitants lived in Imeû, out of which 82 per cent were Catholics and 17 per cent Calvinists. Canonical language was always Hungarian in both churches. In the 1950's bilingual masses were established in the Catholic church but at present they are again carried out only in Hungarian. In 1947 some Calvinist families were deported to Hungary, hence in 1991 Calvinists formed only 6 per cent of its population. Two rows of benches in the church are permanently vacant as a sign of solidarity with deported families. Lately both church communities are less reserved and in some spheres they even cooperate. They coordinate the time of masses, participate in other religious masses and ceremonies to attract more followers.

At the beginning of this century there was only a Hungarian church school in the village in which after the constitution of Czechoslovakia Slovak language was taught 2 hours weekly. In the 1920's a state Slovak school was established there. However the church dissuaded believers from attending the state school. In 1944 the church schools were cancelled and there were two state basic schools which taught Slovak and Hungarian. The Hungarian school was cancelled due to small number of pupils and up to now nobody asked for its re-establishment. Since 1971 several pupils attend this kind of school in the next village. Nearly all children attend Slovak school regardless of their parents' nationality (they regard the teaching process here to be on a good level).

There is only one kindergarten in the village and the parents apply in a written form for the language in which education of their child should be carried out. Imeûlians expect the school and kindergarten to teach or improve the acquisition of Slovak language. Parents consider fluency in Slovak language an important condition for broader professional assertion of their children. Excellent acquisition of

Fig. 3. Common work at threshing corn in the 1940's.

Slovak language represents for them greater life surveillance and they say: "Who knows what's going to happen..."

Stratification of the village community according to property and social status was closely linked with religious faith in the first half of this century. Calvinists belonged to the rich strata of Imeûians. In 1930 they formed hardly one sixth of the inhabitants and they owned two fifths of the cataster. Especially poor Slovak Catholic families migrated for job. The misery of Catholics was increased by a greater number of children and division of inherited property by equal share to each child. Calvinists used to restrict natality.

Ethnic distinction of inhabitants was also very closely linked with religious faith. At the beginning of this century Slovaks were mostly Catholics and Hungarians were Calvinists. Under the influence of the strong Hungarianization in Austro-Hungarian Monarchy many Slovaks reported Hungarian nationality though they could not speak Hungarian very well. This might be the reason why Calvinists considered themselves "genuine Hungarians". They used to call local Catholics "Tóts" (Slovaks) irrespective of the language they spoke. In time of the estate reform in the 1920's it was convenient to report Slovak nationality. After the annexation by Hungary, with the exception of one family, they all reported Hungarian nationality. After deportation of some Hungarian families in 1947 about 60 Slovak families came to the village from Romania and Hungary but they did not settle there.

In 1991 the number of inhabitants was 2 282, out of which 48 per cent declare Slovak and 52 per cent Hungarian nationality. According to statistical data in the last decades and the opinion of the majority of the population, the village is being gradually Hungarianized.

At present ethnic consciousness of the inhabitants is mostly indifferent. Many inhabitants cannot clearly define their ethnicity or they come from a mixed marriage and acquired plural ethnic consciousness. Generally accepted communicative language is Hungarian. It is difficult for a stranger to find out what ethnicity the villagers declared as they all speak Hungarian. Villagers do not consider this fact important or necessary.

In ethnically mixed marriages it is essential to distinguish whether both partners have the same religion or different. Up to the 1950's they preferred to marry a partner of the same religion. The ethnicity factor was mostly secondary in comparison with religion. Catholics were looking for a marriage partner in their own village and also in its vicinity, as well Hungarian as Slovak. When they were of the same religion, they were tolerant towards eth-

Fig. 4. Many vineyards and gardens behind family houses were changed into profitable plastic greenhouses for cultivating vegetables (1992).

nically mixed marriages, especially when they were both poor. Calvinists were strongly endogamic in their religion. As they had narrow possibility of partner selection within the village, they focused on southern Calvinistic localities with Hungarian population. Till the 1930's there was no marriage partners of the other religion. Later when the Calvinistic family did not have a male offspring, they accepted a Catholic son-in-law, but the socially handicapped to secure the dominant position of the wife's family – in religion, language and ethnicity. After 1945 ethnically mixed marriages were more favoured as they feared a possible deportation to Hungary. At present ethnically mixed marriages are quite common. Marriage partners of different religion are more frequent too and religion succession model according to sex is applied: girls inherit mother's religion and boys their father's.

Little attention was paid to ethnicity in the family relations – at present "ethnically pure" families do practically not occur. Today the villagers very often do not know what nationality their relatives report and they only assume it according to the origin of their ancestors, religion and influence of relatives-in-law. That the family was being Hungarianized can be assumed from e.g. the fact that Hungarian speaking people of middle and older age use Slovak terms for denoting relatives in the generation of their parents and grandparents. The attitude of Slovaks toward their ethnicity is more lax. They know their "Slovak roots", but are tolerant to the decision of their offsprings from mixed marriages to declare Hungarian nationality of the children. Hungarian nationality of their children is more frequent in families where one of the partners is a Calvinist.

Exaggerated declaration of ethnicity is rejected in Imeû and a pragmatic view is preferred: "What difference does it make to be Hungarian or Slovak when your bowl is empty and your backside naked." Memories of activities of their ancestors in demonstrating their own ethnicity and in politics are not transferred within the family. It is of no importance to them and they sometimes even wish to forget them. E.g. during the Hungarian occupation of southern Slovakia all Imeû population declared Hungarian nationality. There were "no Slovaks" with the exception of one family, whose breadwinner did not hide this fact and therefore he had a lot of troubles with Hungarian authorities. When I verified this fact with his grandson he knew nothing about it, he was surprised and proud of it.

But the behaviour of some concrete persons is well known because the local chronicler recorded it together with the description of historical events in the chronicle. Offsprings of these people as well as other villagers knew

Fig. 5. Old family cellars in private vineyards (1992).

this fact and referred to the Chronicle. This fact attests the influence of written records on historical and ethnic consciousness of the public.

Family traditions are more respected in the families of Hungarians-Calvinists. Some of them know their pedigree back to the fifth generation and also important events in their lives. Calvinists have also greater respect of family and memories (but it can be due to their contemporary minority feeling in the village).

Groups of neighbours in the investigated village had less space for traditional neighbour activities than in other villages. Stratification according to property formed a certain barrier in developing equal neighbour relations. Property had greater influence on neighbour relations than ethnicity. Nowadays neighbour activities are of the same character as in other villages. Also some traditional activities in the groups of neighbours are maintained and involve all villagers (e.g. keeping the custom of presenting natural produce for wedding banquet).

It is true of cooperative groups' activities in the between-war period that their relations were more influenced by property and social status of their members than by ethnicity. Many activities, which were done in other localities in the form of reciprocal help, were here replaced by cheap labour of agricultural labourers who adapted their language and culture to their employers. Many cooperative chances vanished due to collectivization of agriculture and improvement of household equipment. A renewal of cooperative relations came in the 70's in aspects of family business with cultivating vegetables in individually owned gardens. During the last two years the cooperation (especially reciprocal exchange of manual labour among cooperants) even increased due to economic recession and fewer possibilities of disposal with financial means. Cooperative groups are formed from relatives and neighbours, friends and colleagues. The criterion of ethnicity is not applied in cooperative relations. Common interest – to achieve greater prosperity – has become dominant in cooperation and it suppresses other factors of forming social relation.

Following the investigation of the effect of factors on life and ethnic consciousness, I would like to underline the role of personality (local authority). Both eye-witnesses and the chronicle state that it was the local Catholic priest who had the greatest merit on Hungarianization of Imeû in the 1930's. He preached only in Hungarian, imposed wearing of "Hungarian folk costume" to church, forced Slovak Catholics to send children to Hungarian church school. Before the arrival of Horthy's army he aggravated tense relations in the village to such an extent that the mayor of the village was killed and the teacher of the Slovak school fled away and thus rescued himself (Kronika: 23–26).

The question is to what extent this information from the inhabitants is objective, and whether these events have not been, in the due course of time, so-called "folklorized", though it could be unconscious distortion caused by a longer period of time. On the other hand it can be simple to find and label a man who was resposible for the whole situation in the village and blame him. Unfortunately, at present it is impossible to verify the events by both sides.

It is a matter of fact that especially in the first half of the 20th century population was less informed about happenings in society and citizen rights. The representatives and local authorities could more influence the behaviour of the inhabitants (by informing or not informing, by misinformation and by their own example). This was true in the case of teacher, priest, notary, registrar, chronicler etc.

The change of ethnicity respectively ethnic consciousness of an individual during his life forms a second problem worth of deeper study. In the investigated village break-through situations occurred several times during the last seventy years when the inhabitants for different reasons asserted so-called situational ethnicity (Okamura 1981). When the social and political situation was stabilized they returned or did not return to previously declared ethnicity. The reason for manifestation of another ethnicity than the one an individual was innerly identified with, was his personal ambition (possibility to gain property, effort to achieve a function, to be accepted by members of some social groups). Another reason was their fear of repressions if they did not comply actual political regime. I have also met people who changed their ethnicity so that they could peacefully do their jobs or make use of their talent and skills (e.g. at organizing cultural undertakings) that is in all political regimes.

Slovaks in Imeû "succumbed" Hungarian surrounding in this century. They spoke both languages, what predestined them to adapt to a partner who spoke only Hungarian (in a mixed marriage). In the past and even nowadays Hungarian language provides greater possibility of communication in the nearest vicinity. Aged people who speak only Hungarian did not feel it necessary (nor had the possibility to do so) to learn and speak Slovak.

Old settlers – Slovaks and also those who later settled or married here, were mostly poor. This fact caused their submissive position towards other inhabitants. Marrying a Hungarian partner improved their economic position and social prestige of newcomers but their Slovak ethnic identity gradually ceased.

Changes of borders and political systems caused changes of national identity of Imeû inhabitants. Changes in declaring nationality on the principle of political and economic convenience were common in the whole area of southern Slovakia. This trend occurred in the late 19th century as well as in this century (Šutaj 1992: 165). Hence the factor of ethnicity is not determinant in establishing social (family, kinship, friendship, cooperative, etc.) relations in the community and their function, but rather religion, social status and character of partners are preferred.

At present Imeû inhabitants, both Slovaks and Hungarians, are afraid of the further political development. They consider the present mutual relations between Slovaks and Hungarians as satisfactory and tolerant and a nice example of their cohabitation. It is not a secret that they disapprove to be a constant object of political quarrels. It seems to them that too much attention is paid to the problems of minorities what deteriorates the attitudes of inhabitants from other regions towards them. They have a certain ethnic or rather regional complex of inferiority. A young Slovak woman expressed her feelings: "When visiting the Czech republic I, Slovak citizen, am blamed for the disintegration of the Czechoslovak republic; in Slovakia we are regarded as Hungarians (coming from the southern regions); and in Hungary they label us by a nickname "Tóts" (meaning Slovaks). We are not hurting anybody and nobody likes us!"

When summarizing the factors affecting ethnic consciousness I can state that the cohabitation of ethnics and ethnicity (especially its changes, official declaration and manifestation) were most radically influenced by socio-economic and political changes, macroprocesses with wider social validity. Activities of informal groups were guided towards finding such a model of behaviour which would secure further survival of local community members and if possible, tolerant, were peaceful cohabitation. Complicated and manifold family kinship and neighbour alliances among the inhabitants of the village helped consolidation (e.g. people could not remember a conflict among villagers which would be motivated by ethnicity unless this attitude was incited and supported by tense social situation).

Local representatives and people of natural authority had a certain impact on the life of ethnically mixed local community. This happened especially in the period of political changes or tense political situations. Historical changes also renders an opportunity to fulfil personal ambitions.

References

Jakubíková, Kornélia 1993: Je etnická identifikácia funkciou jazyka? (Is Ethnic Identification the Function of Language?) In: *Slovenský národopis*: 60–64.

Kronika obce Imeû (Imeû Village Chronicle). Archives of Local Council in Imeû.

Žudel, Juraj 1992: Vývoj osídlenia a národnostnej štruktúry obyvateûstva okresu Komárno do roku 1918 (Development of the Settlement and Ethnic Structure in Komárno District till 1918). In: *Etnokultúrny vývoj na južnom Slovensku*: 13–26.

Okamura, J. Y. 1981: Situational Ethnicity. *Ethnic and Racial Studies*, vol. 4, no. 4: 452–465.

Podolák, Ján – Paríková, Magdaléna 1992: Stručná charakteristika skúmaných obcí (Brief Characteristics of Researched Localities). In: *Etnokultúrny vývoj na južnom Slovensku*: 41–54.

Suppan, Arnold – Henberger, Valeria 1992: States and Minorities in the Danube Region (1945–1990). In: *Minorities in Politics*: 61–72.

Škovierová, Zita 1992: Sociálne skupiny a etnická príslušnosť v Imeli (Social Groups and Ethnicity in Imeû village). In: *Etnokultúrny vývoj na južnom Slovensku*: 55–63.

Šutaj, Štefan 1992: Changes of National Identity in Historical Development. In: *Minorities in Politics*: 182–187.

Ungarndeutsche in Geretsried

Balázs Balogh

Balogh, Balázs 1994: Ungarndeutsche in Geretsried – Ethnologia Europaea 24: 59–66.

Nach dem 2. Weltkrieg, zwischen 1945 und 48 ereilte mehr als 200 000 Ungarndeutsche das Schicksal der Zwangsumsiedlung. Auf Pusztavám in Transdanubien, dessen Einwohner fast zu 100% deutschstämmig waren, wartete die gleiche Erfahrung. Die aus Pusztavám herausgekommenen Ungarndeutschen und ihre Nachkommen wohnen grösstenteils in Geretsried in Bayern. Hier in Geretsried führten wir 1992 eine Feldforschung aus. Um auf diesem Gebiet gesammelte Erfahrungen auch auf die Erforschung des Lebens der in Bayern verstreuten Ungarndeutschen auszudehnen, versandten wir bayernweit 300 Fragebögen. Unser Ziel war es, die Akkulturation der Geretsrieder Ungarndeutschen aufzuzeichnen und das in Bayern gesammelte Material mit den Geretsrieder Erfahrungen zu vergleichen. Die wesentliche Frage in unserer Untersuchung bestand also darin, inwiefern in welchen Teilen und durch welche Einflüsse sich die während des 300-jährigen deutschungarischen Zusammenlebens sich herausgebildete ungarndeutsche Identität und Lebensweise nach der Übersiedlung in die neue Umgebung, geändert hat. Mit der neuen lebensweise veränderten sich ihre Beziehungsstruktur, Materialkultur, Identität, sie nahmen neuen Sitten von den anderen ausgesiedelten Deutschen und den Bayern an. Die Bewahrung der Tradition ist bei den in Geretsried zusammenlebenden Puzstavámer wesentlich stärker als bei den in Bayern verstreuten anderen Ungarndeutschen.

Balázs Balogh, Institute of Ethnology, Hungarian Academy of Sciences, P.O. Box 29, H-1250 Budapest, Hungary.

Im Winter 1944/45 floh ein Teil der ungarndeutschen Bevölkerung aus ihren Dörfern vor den anrückenden sowjetischen Truppen in den Westen. Viele von ihnen kehrten nie mehr nach Ungarn zurück. Auf die Daheimgebliebenen wartete die organisierte Aussiedlung. Nach dem 2. Weltkrieg, zwischen 1945 und 48 ereilte mehr als 200 000 Ungarndeutsche das unmenschliche Schicksal der Zwangsumsiedlung. Wie in vielen Ländern Europas, so wurde auch in Ungarn im Sinne internationaler Vereinbarungen die Vertreibung der deutschen nationalen Minderheiten wegen der sogenannten Kollektivschuld durchgeführt. Auf Pusztavám in Transdanubien, dessen Einwohner fast zu 100% deutschstämmig waren, wartete die gleiche schreckliche Erfahrung. Ein Teil der Bevölkerung wanderte aus, ein anderer Teil wurde umgesiedelt und manche von ihnen – in ihrer Sprache schon stark an das Ungarische angeglichen – leben noch heute in Pusztavám. Die aus Pusztavám auf diese oder jene Art herausgekommenen Ungarndeutschen und ihre Nachkommen wohnen grösstenteils in Geretsried, einer kleinen Stadt in Bayern.

Geretsried liegt 40 km südlich von München auf einer schmalen Landzunge zwischen den Flüssen Loisach und Isar. Noch während des 2. Weltkrieges stand kein Wohnhaus an der Stelle des heutigen Städtchens, aber ein kilometerlanger Bunkerkomplex, der als Waffenlager und als Munitionsfabrik verwendet wurde. Diese Gebäude wurden im Frühjahr 1945 bei einem Luftangriff der Alliierten teilweise beschädigt. In die nach dem Krieg leer stehenden Bunker und in die Baracken der Zwangsarbeiter zogen die ersten, vor der Front fliehenden, heimatlos gewordenen deutschen Volksgruppen ein. Sie waren es, die unter den aus Pusztavám stammenden Familien, die bei den umliegenden Bauern einlogiert worden waren und dort arbeiteten, die Nachricht verbreiteten, dass in den Baracken und Bunkern

Fig. 1. Teil des Bunkerkomplexes; zur Zeit Wohnhäuser.

Wohnmöglichkeiten vorhanden seien. Es charakterisiert das Zusammengehörigkeitsgefühl der Ungarndeutschen aus Pusztavám, dass sich die Familien auch in der Diaspora gegenseitig suchten. In den 50er Jahren zogen zum Beispiel 77 Pusztavámer Familien in das aufstrebende Geretsried. Freilich kamen auch andere Landsleute in grosser Anzahl in dieser Zeit hinzu.

Der Zusammenhalt der Deutschen aus Pusztavám war jedoch so gross, dass sie innerhalb von Geretsried zusammenzogen und ein eigenes Viertel bildeten, das sie Jakob Bleyer-Siedlung nannten. Diese Wohngegend – wo die Pusztavámer Ungarndeutschen sozusagen wie auf einem Dorf in der Stadt leben – wird von den anderen Geretsrieder Volksdeutschen nicht Jakob Bleyer-Siedlung genannt, sondern einfach »Ungarnsiedlung«. Damit wollen sie nicht die Nationalität der Deutschen aus Ungarn bezeichnen, sondern deren Herkunftsland. Da es in Geretsried keine bayerischen Einheimischen gibt, ist jeder ein »Einwanderer«. Es ist besonders interessant, dass in einer Siedlung vier grosse, aus verschiedenen Ländern und aus unterschiedlichen Kulturen kommenden deutschen Volksgruppen aufeinandertreffen. (Aus Ungarn, Schlesien, Sudetenland und Siebenbürgen.) Die Stadt selbst – sie hat heute um die 20 000 Einwohner – liegt in einer bayerischen Umgebung.

Bezüglich der Anzahl der in Bayern lebenden Ungarndeutschen kennen wir nur vorsichtige Schätzungen, die uns von ungefähr 30 000 berichten. Die Geretsrieder Gemeinde verdient auch deshalb unsere Aufmerksamkeit, weil der Grossteil der aus Ungarn vertriebenen circa 200 000 Deutschen sich in Baden-Württemberg niedergelassen hat. Die uns zur Verfügung stehende Statistik zeigt auf, dass in Bayern bis 1948 insgesamt 103 Gemeinden Ungarndeutsche aufgenommen haben. (Selbstverständlich gab es in den vergangenen Jahrzehnten viele gesellschaftliche Veränderungen, so dienen diese Daten nur zur Orientierung.) Ausserdem stammen die in einem Ort sich niedergelassenen Ungarndeutschen aus ganz verschiedenen Regionen Ungarns. Die Folgen dieser grossen Streuung sind die relativ schnelle Assimilierung und die Tatsache, dass in den 90er Jahren nur noch in Geretsried eine geschlossene, kompakte ungarndeutsche Gemeinde in Bayern zu finden ist.

Hier in Geretsried führte ich 1992 unter den Deutschen aus Pusztavám eine Feldforschung und eine Fragebogenaktion durch. Die circa 1 000 Personen zählende Gemeinde der Ungarndeutschen, die hauptsächlich aus Pusztavám stammt, ist zur einen Hälfte katholisch, zur anderen evangelisch.

Um meine, auf diesem Gebiet gesammelten Erfahrungen auch auf die Erforschung des Le-

Fig. 2. Pusztavámer in seiner Wohnung in Geretsried; links kleine ungarische Fahne; rechts an der Wand Panorama von Budapest.

bens der in Bayern verstreuten Ungarndeutschen auszudehnen, versandte ich bayernweit 300 Fragebögen. Es kamen mehr als 100 Fragebögen ausgefüllt zurück. Die Rücksender wurden zwischen 1903 und 1953 geboren und sind überwiegend männlich. Mein Ziel war es, die Akkulturation der Geretsrieder Ungarndeutschen aufzuzeichnen und das in Bayern gesammelte Material mit den Geretsrieder Erfahrungen zu vergleichen, selbstverständlich unter Berücksichtigung der unterschiedlichen Konfessionen, Berufe, Geschlechter und Altersklassen.

Die wesentliche Frage in meiner Untersuchung bestand also darin, inwiefern die während des 300-jährigen deutsch-ungarischen Zusammenlebens sich herausgebildete ungarndeutsche Identität und Lebensweise nach der Übersiedlung in die neue Umgebung, in welchen Teilen und durch welche Einflüsse sich geändert hat. Deshalb nahm ich nach Möglichkeit an den gemeinschaftlichen Festen der Ungarndeutschen teil, untersuchte ihre Beziehungsstruktur, beobachtete ihre Materialkultur und vieles anderes mehr.

Der interessanteste, aber psychologisch meist problematische Teil der Forschung war die persönlich oder durch den Fragebogen gestellte Frage nach der Nationalität. Aufgrund der in den Fragebögen gegebenen Antworten ist es typisch für die gemischte Identität, dass sich die betroffenen Menschen, unterschiedliche Reihenfolgen aufstellend, sich gleichzeitig als Ungarndeutsche, Deutsche und Bayern bezeichneten. In den meisten Fällen (40–40%) bekannten sie sich als Ungarndeutsche und Deutsche. Oft löste die Frage eine seelische Erschütterung bei den Befragten aus. Sie sahen sich mit einer Frage konfrontiert, über die viele selbst nicht gerne sprechen. Interessanterweise unterschieden sich die diesbezüglichen Antworten der bayernweit verschickten Fragebögen wesentlich von den Antworten aus Geretsried. Die aus Pusztavám stammenden Mitglieder der Geretsrieder Gemeinschaft benannten sich alle – unabhängig von Alter, Geschlecht, Beruf und Religion – als Ungarndeutsche. Dem gegenüber bewegten sich die Antworten der verstreuten Ungarndeutschen zwischen zwei Extremen. Manche fanden es als unangebracht, dass sich ein ungarischer Wissenschaftler nach ihrer Identität und Kultur erkundigt. Beispiele diesbezüglicher Antworten sind:

»Die deutsche-bayerische-ungarndeutsche-schwäbische Nation wurde aus Ungarn vertrieben, nicht ausgesiedelt. Diese in Ungarn als 'nem is igazi német, csak sváb', also, kein echter Deutscher, nur ein Schwabe verachtete deutsche Volksgruppe wurde ja auch nicht nach Bayern oder Schwaben oder gar in ein 'sonstiges' Land, sondern nach Deutschland verjagt. Damals wusste man noch in Ungarn, woher sie kamen, dorthin sollten sie also wieder zurückgehen!«

Und der Zitierte schrieb noch ein Sprichwort dazu: »Ihr kamt mit einem Bündel, mit einem Bündel sollt ihr gehen.« Dieses Sprichwort war leider die Losung der Aussiedlungen zwischen 1945–48 in Ungarn.

Diese in ihrer nationalen Identität verletzten Menschen nannten sich immer Deutsche oder Bayern, aber keinesfalls Ungarndeutsche. Psychologisch ist diese Reaktion verständlich, da schon allein die Aussiedlung inhuman ist, jedoch paarte sich die Aussiedlung aus Ungarn häufig mit physischen Leiden. Es ist offensichtlich, dass das furchtbare Erlebnis der Vertreibung die Vertriebenen dazu bewegt hat, sowohl ihre Abstammung aus Ungarn als auch ihre Bezeichnung als Ungarndeutsche absichtlich zu vergessen. Eine hierzu bezeichnende Begründung ist: »Die Vertreibung ist endgültig, darum bin ich deutsch.« Das Gegenteil der obengenannten Gruppe bilden jene, die sich als Ungarndeutsche bezeichnen und sich gerne an die alte Heimat erinnern. Ein rührendes Beispiel dazu ist die Antwort eines 1912 geborenen Mannes, der schrieb: »Selbst nach 47 Jahren schlägt unser Herz rot-weiss-grün.«

Im Grossen und Ganzen kann man also feststellen, dass das Identitätsbewusstsein der zerstreuten ungarndeutschen Ausgesiedelten am meisten von ihren Aussiedlungserlebnissen geprägt ist: ob sie nun vor dem Krieg flohen, oder aus der Gefangenschaft zurückkehrten, wann und unter welchen Umständen sie ausgesiedelt wurden, beziehungsweise wie die neue Umgebung beschaffen war, usw.

Den in Geretsried zusammengebliebenen Menschen aus Pusztavám jedoch bot die ungarndeutsche Identität eine aus dem Zusammengehörigkeitsgefühl entstandene Sicherheit in den letzten vier Jahrzehnten und auch heute noch. Es ist also kein zufall, dass in Bayern nur in Geretsried eine ungarndeutsche Tradition bewahrende Trachtengruppe gegründet wurde.

Die Feste haben eine grosse Bedeutung in der Gemeinschaft. An diesen Veranstaltungen versuchen alle nach Möglichkeit teilzunehmen. Die Kinder werden von den Eltern auf diese Feste mitgebracht, für die Jugend sind sie eine gute Gelegenheit zur Paarbildung, so besteht auch innerhalb der ungarndeutschen Gemeinde die Möglichkeit der Partnerfindung. Die von den Geretsriedern besuchten und teilweise organisierten Feste sind folgende:

1. Münchener Schwabenball (am ersten Samstag nach dem Dreikönigstag)
2. Geretsrieder Schwabenball (am 4. Samstag im Januar)
3. Fasching (im Februar)
4. Osterratschen (für die Kinder)
5. Maibaumfest
6. Sonnwendfeier (am 21.6.)
7. Geretsrieder Sommerfest (von zehn Tage Dauer inkl. den ersten Sonntag im August)
8. Siedlungsfest (am 2. Samstag im September)
9. Traubenball (am 1. oder 2. Samstag im Oktober)
10. Tag der Heimat (am 1. Sonntag im Oktober, das Fest wird wechselweise von ausgesiedelten Deutschen aus verschiedenen Orten veranstaltet. Die Ungarndeutschen kommen alle vier Jahre an die Reihe.)
11. Die Jahresabschlussfeier (Ende November oder Anfang Dezember)
12. Nikolausfeier am 6.12. für Kinder.

Die meisten dieser Feste sind neueren Datums, die nur in Geretsried von den Pusztavámern gefeiert werden. So zum Beispiel das Siedlungsfest, das sie 1987 von den Bayern übernommen haben. Die Sonnwendfeier halten sie zusammen mit den Sudetendeutschen ab, weil sie diesen Brauch von den Sudetendeutschen erlernt haben. Meist ist der Höhepunkt eines Festes das Auftreten der Trachtengruppe. Die Pusztavámer sind sehr stolz auf ihre Gruppe. Die in Bayern verstreuten Ungarndeutschen kennen laut Umfrageergebnis überall die Geretsrieder Trachtengruppe. In der Tanzgruppe des Trachtenvereins gibt es eine Senioren-, Jugend- und Kindergruppe.

Fig. 3. Tanzende Kindergruppe in Pusztavámer Festtracht in Geretsried.

Die Tanzgruppen proben einmal in der Woche, im Haus eines begeisterten Veranstalters, der selbst auch die Tänze lehrt. Unter den Tänzen gibt es noch einige authentische aus Pusztavám, die der Tanzlehrer noch von seinem Grossvater gelernt hatte.

Die enthusiastische Teilnahme an den ungarndeutschen Veranstaltungen ist im Falle der in Bayern verstreuten Ungarndeutschen kaum vorhanden. Ich nahm selbst an vielen Festen der in Bayern verstreut lebenden Ungarndeutschen teil, wo mich meine Erfahrungen zu der Überzeugung brachten, dass für die ältere Generation die Veranstaltungen von grosser Bedeutung sind, während die Nachkriegsgeneration überhaupt nicht präsent ist. Das bedeutet also, dass sich die Kinder und Enkelkinder der Ausgesiedelten in das Bayerische integriert haben. Die ältere erste Generation ist teilweise ausgestorben oder kann nur kaum oder gar nicht an den Veranstaltungen teilnehmen. Ein gutes Beispiel dafür ist der ungarndeutsche Schwabenball in München. Dieser Ball wird schon seit einigen Jahren gemeinsam mit den Banater Schwaben organisiert, da im letzten Jahrzehnt die Zahl der teilnehmenden Ungarndeutschen so radikal gesunken ist, dass nicht einmal die Hälfte des Salvatorkellers ausgefüllt werden konnte. Das Durchschnittsalter der Teilnehmenden ist zwischen 55 und 60 Jahren. Die zweite, aber besonders die dritte Generation bekennt sich beinahe ausnahmslos zu den Bayern. Nach der Meinung sämtlicher Jugendlicher sind die ungarndeutschen Bälle und weitere Veranstaltungen altmodische Erscheinungen, nur zum belächeln. Ein kleiner Teil der Jugendlichen besucht diese Veranstaltungen nur um der Eltern und Grosseltern Willen. Das Ergebnis meiner Gespräche sowohl mit den Älteren als auch mit den Jüngeren wies darauf hin, dass sich auch die alte Sprache der Ungarndeutschen völlig verändert und innerhalb eines Generationswechsels ins Bayerische verwandelt hat. Dieser Assimilationsvorgang kennzeichnet die Kultur der Ungarndeutschen in Bayern im Wandel der Generationen. Eine Ausnahme dabei bilden die Geretsrieder, deren ungarndeutsche Identität sich bis in die dritte Generation vererbte. Hier nehmen alle ungeachtet ihres Alters, Geschlechts usw. an den gemeinsamen Feiern teil.

Bei der Untersuchung der Beziehungsstruktur der bayerischen Ungarndeutschen stellte sich heraus, dass die in der ersten Hälfte dieses Jahrhunderts Geborenen einen ganz engen Kontakt mit den restlichen Ungarndeutschen in der alten Heimat aufrecht erhalten, in fast 90% der Fälle mit Verwandten. Aber auch der Kontakt mit den Freunden und Bekannten ist bedeutend. Beinahe jeder Befragte steht in regelmässigem Briefwechsel mit Ungarndeutschen in Ungarn, aber die intensivste Form der Kontakte ist der persönliche Besuch, der meistens gegenseitig ist.

Diese gegenseitigen Besuche begannen schon in den 60er Jahren und wurden durch die Ereignisse in den 80er Jahren in Osteuropa immer häufiger. Heutzutage fahren ungefähr 70% der befragten Ungarndeutschen jährlich oder alle zwei Jahre nach Ungarn. Die Zahl derer, die nur aus touristischen Gründen oder überhaupt nie nach Ungarn fahren, ist

Fig. 4. Pusztavámer in seinem Weinkeller in Geretsried.

sehr gering. Die Ungarndeutschen in Bayern suchen in der neuen Heimat auch die Gesellschaft von einander, 80% trifft sich regelmässig mit anderen Ungarndeutschen.

Auch in dieser Hinsicht bilden die Geretsrieder eine Ausnahme. Der Kontakt zu den Menschen in ihrem Heimatdorf in Ungarn ist noch intensiver. Diese Beziehungen wurden seit der Wende in Ungarn auf Gemeindeebene fortgesetzt. Zu bestimmten Festen der Gemeinde fahren die Ungarndeutschen aus Geretsried mit Bussen nach Pusztavám und umgekehrt.

Was die materielle Kultur betrifft, ist es augenfällig, dass es nur sehr wenige kontinuierliche Kulturelemente aus der Zeit vor der Aussiedlung bis heute gibt. Das ist nicht überraschend, da die Umsiedlung oder die Flucht die Mitnahme des gewohnten materiellen Umfeldes nach Bayern ausgeschlossen hat. Die Umsiedler mussten nach dem Kriege sozusagen aus dem Nichts ihre Existenz begründen und ihre materielle Umgebung neu erschaffen. Das Verlassen der Heimat ging mit einem beträchtlichen Wechsel der Lebensform einher.

Vor dem Krieg lebten die meisten in Pusztavám von der Landwirtschaft, jedoch hatte das Dorf eine bedeutende Handwerkerschicht und es arbeiteten einige in dem in der Nähe des Dorfes um die Jahrhundertwende eröffneten Bergwerk. Diese Beschäftigungen konnten die Ungarndeutschen in Geretsried nicht fortführen. Die Umsiedler, deren grösster Teil heute Rentner sind, und deren Nachkommen fanden in den Fabriken der Stadt und in der Umgebung Arbeit, oder kamen im Dienstleistungsgewerbe unter.

Alltagstracht gibt es nicht mehr, und auch der Sonntagsstaat wird nur noch von der Trachtengruppe zur feierlichen Anlässen aufgetragen. Diese Trachten sind nicht im Privatbesitz, sondern gehören dem Verein. Die Feste aber, in deren Rahmen die Trachtengruppe auftritt und in der alten Tracht tanzt, spielen eine wichtige Rolle im Leben der Geretsrieder Ungarndeutschen. Diese Gelegenheiten sind Erinnerungen an die alte Heimat.

Die Auswahl der sogenannten Erinnerungsstücke ist rein zufällig und hing eher von der emotionalen Bindung als von rationalen Überlegungen ab. Unter den Erinnerungsstücken finden wir Spinnräder, Ziehharmonikas, Wandschoner, Kleidertruhen, Perlen und Häkeldecken. Zu den wenigen charakteristischen Erinnerungsstücken gehören die Familienfotos, die Handarbeiten, die Bibel und die verschiedenen Familiendokumente. In dieser Hinsicht gibt es keine gravierenden Unterschiede zwischen den bayerischen und den Geretsrieder Ungarndeutschen.

Unter den grossen Veränderungen des Lebensstils ereilte die Esskultur vielleicht die geringste Wandlung. In dieser Hinsicht sind die Unterschiede zwischen den bayerischen Ungarndeutschen und den Geretsriedern am kleinsten. Eine Speiseordnung für die Woche kann man nur bei einigen wenigen sehr alten Menschen feststellen. Jene die sich noch auf die traditionelle Weise ernähren, haben am Montag, Mittwoch und Freitag Teigtag, und an den weiteren Tagen gibt es auch Fleischgerichte. Variiert wird der Montag mit Kartoffelmahlzeiten, der Freitag mit Fisch, Bohnen und

Knödel. Sonntags ist bis heute die »Sonntagssuppe« unerlässlich, eine Fleischsuppe.

Die verschiedenen Feiertage haben ihre charakteristischen Mahlzeiten, die nicht nur bei den Geretsriedern, sondern auch bei den anderen bayerischen Ungarndeutschen auf den Tisch kommen. Das wichtigste vielleicht dabei ist, dass die traditionellen Gerichte, die auch in der ungarischen Küche vorkommen, mit aus Ungarn mitgebrachten Gewürzen zubereitet werden. So kommt es häufig vor, besonders in Geretsried, dass aus dem hier in den Metzgereien gekauften Fleisch zu Hause Würste hergestellt werden, auf die noch in Ungarn gekannte Art.

Sehr beliebt sind in ihren Kreisen das Széklergulasch, Krautwickeln, Letscho und Zwetschgenknödel, die verschiedenen Paprikaschs, und es lohnt sich zu bemerken, dass ausser den Exilungarn nur die Ungarndeutschen wissen, was ein Pörkölt eigentlich ist. Selbstverständlich ist auch ein Einfluss der bayerischen und europäischen Küche in der ungarndeutschen Esskultur vorhanden, doch im Wesentlichen unterscheidet sie sich nicht von der ungarischen.

Bei den Geretsriedern muss jedoch noch die wichtige Rolle des selbstgekelterten Weines erwähnt werden. Der selbstgekelterte Wein ist das ausgeprägteste Symbol der Pusztavámer-ungarndeutschen Identitaet, das sie nicht nur von den Bayern, sondern auch von den aus Ungarn und anderswo ausgesiedelten Deutschen unterscheidet. Das Leben der aus dem Weingebiet Mór kommenden Pusztavámer durchdrang der Weinbau so sehr, dass sie auch in ihrer neuen Umgebung, wo keine Weinreben wachsen, aus gekauften Trauben Wein herstellen. Deshalb sind die Pusztavámer nicht nur in Geretsried berühmt. Sie halten sogar ein Weinlesefest ab, auf dem auch gekaufte Trauben aufgetischt werden. Ihre Anhänglichkeit zum Weinbau ist auch an Äusserlichkeiten zu erkennen: Reben schmücken das Wappen von Pusztavám, die Grabsteine in Geretsried, und auch das Deckblatt des Heimatbuches, usw.

Das bisherige zusammenfassend können wir folgendes feststellen: die Bewahrung der Traditionen ist bei den in Geretsried zusammenlebenden Pusztavámer wesentlich stärker als bei den in Bayern verstreuten anderen Ungarndeutschen. Das Geretsrieder Beispiel zeigt die traditionserhaltende Kraft der Gemeinschaft auf. In einer fremden Umgebung verstärkte sich das Wir-Gefühl: "Wir sind Pusztavámer, ihr nicht."

Diese ungarndeutsche Identität ist noch immer so prägend, dass bei gemischten Ehen der auswärtige Partner meistens in die Gemeinschaft der Pusztavámer, in die Ungarnsiedlung zieht, wobei er sich auch teilweise assimiliert. Z.B.: Eine bayerische Ehefrau lernt das Kochen der Pusztavámer Gerichte, das Kind ist Mitglied im Trachtenverein usw. Da sie geschlossen zusammenleben, haben sie im Gegensatz zu den anderen Ungarndeutschen bessere Möglichkeiten, ihre gemeinsamen Feste zu veranstalten.

Selbstverständlich veränderte sich mit der Lebensweise auch ihre Kultur, sie nahmen neue Sitten von den anderen ausgesiedelten Deutschen und den Bayern an, aber sie sind stolz auf ihre eigenen authentischen Traditionen und pflegen diese bewusst.

Die Betonung liegt auf bewusst, weil sie erkannten, dass sie in fremder Umgebung auf einander angewiesen waren, und nur mit vereinten Kräften ihre neue Welt leichter aufbauen konnten. Deshalb gründeten sie ihre traditionserhaltenden Vereine, entwickelten die Vorraussetzungen für ihre gemeinschaftlichen Feste, halten bewusst den Kontakt zu den Pusztavámern in Ungarn aufrecht und nehmen aktiv am Leben der Organisationen der in Deutschland gegründeten donauschwäbischen Landsmannschaften teil.

Hoffentlich kann die kleine ungarndeutsche Gemeinschaft noch lange ihre Identität im grossen Bayern bewahren, die durch ein 300-jähriges deutsch-ungarisches Zusammenleben im Karpatenbecken geformt wurde.

Summary

Immediately after World War II – between 1945 and 1948 – more than 200,000 Hungarian Germans (Ungarndeutschen) were made to suffer the inhuman fate of forced resettlement. As was the case in several other European countries, the order of resettlement in Hungary was founded on international agreements drawn up on the basis of the alleged "collective guilt" of German ethnic groups.

The almost entirely German-speaking population of Pusztavám, a village in the Transdanubian region in the west of Hungary, were among those forced to leave their homes. Some simply fled from the village, others were forced to resettle, while the remainder – considerably "Magyarised" in their language – still live in Pusztavám. The majority of those who were forced to leave Pusztavám and their descendants, today live in a small Bavarian town, Geretsried.

The research outlined in this article was based on field work and a questionnaire-survey carried out among the Pusztavám Germans. In order to broaden the scope of my research, I also sent some 300 copies of a questionnaire to other "Ungarndeutsch" families resettled from Hungary to Bavaria. The main purpose of my research was to map the extent of the "acculturalisation" in Geretsried and then to compare these results with those obtained in Bavaria as a whole – paying special attention to the religious denomination, occupation, gender, and age of the communities in question. To this end, I frequently participated in various communal festivities of the "Ungarndeutschen" in Geretsried. I analysed their social interaction and examined their daily diet and material environment. The central question of the research, therefore, was, in what ways and under what influences have the "Ungarndeutschen", after living with Hungarians for 300 years, only to be forcibly resettled almost 50 years ago, changed their identity and ways of living in a foreign environment.

Summarising the results of my research, I would suggest that the Germans from Hungary living together in Geretsried are considerably more anxious to preserve their traditions than other "Ungarndeutsche" scattered all over Bavaria and living in isolation. The example of Geretsried clearly demonstrates what a strong cohesive force a community may exert. In Geretsried the self-identity of the "Ungarndeutschen" became intensified, well expressed in the simple sentence: "We are from Pusztavám but you are not!"

Naturally, the "Ungarndeutschen" in Geretsried changed their culture in accordance with the change in the circumstances of their lives. They acquired new traditions from other Germans resettled from other regions, and also from the host Bavarians, but they are also proud of their own traditions and consciously cultivate them. It is important to emphasise the word "consciously" since they have realised that they are dependent on one another in a foreign environment and that together they are more able to create their new surroundings. That is why they established their tradition-preserving group, creating the necessary conditions for properly organising their communal festivities, and why they consciously foster their relationships with the Germans remaining in Pusztavám, dynamically involving themselves in the activities of the Danube Region Swabian Organisations.

"Mother help me get a good mark in history"

Ethnological Analysis of Wall Inscriptions in the Church of St. Peter and Paul in Osijek (Croatia)

Jasna Čapo Žmegač

Jasna Čapo Žmegač 1994: »Mother help me get a good mark in history«. Ethnological Analysis of Wall Inscriptions in the Church of St. Peter and Paul in Osijek (Croatia). – Ethnologia Europaea 24: 67–76.

The author proposes to analyze messages (prayers) addressed to the Virgin Mary. They are written on the walls of the chapel of Our Lady of Lourdes, which is located in the church of St. Peter and Paul in Osijek (eastern Croatia). The appropriate genre into which these messages can be ranged is discussed and a proposition is reached that they cannot be considered *graffiti*. In the analysis the author compares them to similar messages found at yet another Croatian church and at a church in Alsace, France. The conclusions are reached regarding the age and gender of the authors, the themes and beneficiaries of the prayers, the appellation of the Virgin, and the relationship that the authors establish with her.

Jasna Čapo Žmegač, Ph.D., Institute of Ethnology and Folklore Research, Ulica kralja Zvonimira 17, 41000 Zagreb, Croatia.

A reader might wonder at the title and the subtitle of this text and ask her/himself what kind of a wall inscription is it by which a good mark in history is prayed for, what mother is that? I shall first attempt to make these questions clear. Then I shall present some theoretical assumptions and methodological problems involved in the analysis of data, and finally, the results of the analysis.

Messages addressed to the Virgin, the Mother of God, found in the chapel of Our Lady of Lourdes in the church of St. Peter and Paul in Osijek (eastern Croatia), are the basis for this research. They are written on chapel walls, usually with a ball point pen, in capital or small letters. They cover seven walls of the octogonal chapel (the eighth is the entrance), and extend outside the chapel on the walls to the left and to the right of the entrance. They fill up wall surfaces from the bottom to about two meters' height. Tablets with thanksgivings and requests graved in stone ornate chapel walls, but written messages do not respect them: they appear between and next to them, but also on them, one upon the other, making it sometimes difficult, even impossible, to uncover overlayed messages.

It was not possible to find out when this practice began. The oldest recovered message is from 1972 and represents the minimal lower border of the inception of the writing of wall messages. All inscriptions are addressed to the Virgin or to God, either in the form of a request and/or a thanksgiving. By their content they are a manifestation of popular religiosity, and as a subject of research are related to studying pilgrimages, vows, votive objects or, more generally, relationships that people maintain with saint or divine persons.

Graffiti or public prayers?

Wall inscriptions in Osijek present a rare combination of, on the one hand, a special form of

Fig. 1. The chapel of Our Lady of Lourdes, the church of St. Peter and Paul, Osijek.

expression – a public wall inscription or *graffiti*, and, on the other hand, religious content that is most commonly unrelated to this form. There seems to be no general agreement upon the definition of graffiti. Various definitions usually emphasize only one of their characteristics, assuming that it is the most prominent one. For example, some distinguish them solely according to their formal characteristics as inscriptions and drawings on walls (Lalić 1991: 29–30). The inscriptions from Osijek conform to that criterion.

Other definitions stress the trespassing of a prohibition as a constitutive element in the definition of graffiti. That constituent is in close connection with the definition of graffiti as an act of vandalism (Gamboni 1988: 213, Lalić 1991: 30). The condemnation of graffiti leads to their destruction, in some cases even to persecution of their authors (Billeter 1988). Wall inscriptions from Osijek again conform to this criterion. According to the church staff they damage the church walls and, both by their content and by their positioning, they disturb the sanctity of the place. Therefore, they are regularly wiped out. That is a never ending process, because new authors fill up (imperfectly) erased surfaces, or overwrite existing messages. With several older, still partly visible layers, the walls of the chapel have become a contemporary version of a palimpsest.

However, the Osijek inscriptions are not, like graffiti, a form of public communication practiced by individuals who cannot communicate in a usual and socially accepted way (Lalić 1991: 32, Skasa-Weiss 1988: 208). Namely, the Osijek inscriptions are not addressed to unknown receivers. Although they might reach unknown public – visitors of the church – they aim at being received by a specific receiver – the Virgin.

None of the above mentioned writers has discussed wall inscriptions inside a church as a case of graffiti. However, sacral spaces have frequently represented beloved surfaces for writing various messages. Croatia is no exception to this. Glagolitic[1] inscriptions were written in secular but even more in sacral spaces, especially in the north coastal Croatia during a long period of time between the 10th and 18th centuries[2] (Fučić 1982). Closer in time, we can find inscriptions inside churches and on small sacral objects in the northwestern and eastern Croatia (Horvat 1956, 1975). They probably belong to the 18th century and might represent magic signs for protection or ritual prayers for success in hunting (ibid.).

I propose that inscriptions on the inner walls of the church of St. Peter and Paul in Osijek, although they have some of the most prominent characteristics of graffiti – they are written on the walls, in a public sphere, they result in transgression leading to attempts of the church staff to destroy them, they are anonymous – are still not graffiti.[3] They cannot be considered graffiti for various reasons: first, their receiver is not meant to be an anonymous mass of people living in a big city; second, their messages do not primarily result from an opposition and wish to transgress an interdiction nor from a communication deficit (impossibility of public expression in society); and last but not least, by their contents they are not graffiti. The inscriptions from Osijek are prayers (requests and thanksgivings) of individuals to the Virgin for her interference into their lives. Therefore, in spite of their form, they belong to the same genre as pilgrims' prayers which are found in various pilgrimage churches.

Wall inscriptions as texts

Before embarking on the analysis of texts, it is appropriate to comment shortly on the creation of wall inscriptions and my interpretation of them. It is argued that this study carries the double mark of fictionality – one can be found already at the level of data, and one at the level of their interpretation and analysis.

Prayers aim at communication with the divine with the intention of asking or thanking for a grace, but they also convey a certain understanding of the world of the author, i. e. they can be used as material for research into a person's comprehension of the world and of his/her place in it, specifically with regards to the relationship between a person and divine beings. In that short text, the author reveals his/her thoughts through a certain form – a prayer – which is a certain genre with its conventions of expression. As a conventional type of discourse it influences the communication between an individual and a divine being (cf. Velčić 1991). By its conventions, a prayer mediates human experience and gives it form. Therefore, the object of analysis and interpretation is not just human life but also (or even more) a text about it, a text which, using the conventions of a specific genre, turns a personal discourse into a non-personal, generalized expression, into a sort of fiction. In other words, in the analysis to follow, we shall not reach human lives directly, but indirectly through texts.

The interpretation of data and the writing of a scientific text also involve fictionalization. Ethnology/cultural anthropology has only recently begun to question systematically the processes of interpretation and of writing up

Fig. 2. Hand written messages alternate with graved stone tablets. Both contain a message for the Virgin.

ethnographies. It is posited by one of the proponents of new ethnography that this relatively late questioning "reflects the persistence of an ideology claiming transparency of representation and immediacy of experience" (Clifford 1986: 2). By this ideology the interpretation of culture and the writing about it have been reduced to method: it has been thought that if a researcher disposes with good fieldwork notes and knows how to draw accurate maps, s/he can without difficulties write up the results of the research (ibid.). The critics of that position focus on the making of ethnographic texts, pointing out to their constructed, artificial nature. They refer to ethnographic texts as to fictions (in the sense of "something made or fashioned"), as to partial cultural and historical truths (ibid.: 6–7).

In this sense, it will be taken that the following analysis and the ensuing text will provide only one among a number of possible interpretations, a partial truth in which reality will be both described and made up.

Fig. 3. A couple of examples of prayers: "Mother defend us from the war and return happiness in my life (first name)", or, "Mother please make that I start dating D. B. soon, and that we love each other for a long time."

Comments on the method

One thousand wall inscriptions are the basis of the present analysis. This number encompasses perhaps a majority of existing (legible) inscriptions, assuring that we really have a representative sample. The analysis of inscriptions containing the date (16.5% of cases) indicates that in majority they were written between 1987 and October 1992 (when the data were gathered).

The methodology has been worked out using two French analyses (Fainzang 1991, Herberich-Marx 1991). I have combined the methodology proposed by these two authors making adjustments where the data dictated them and where I judged that they would contribute to the analysis. These differences of method account for the incomparability of certain results obtained in the analyses of Croatian and French data.

I shall present some of the analyses of the data from Osijek comparing them to the analysis of prayers from Trsat[4] (Čapo 1992), and to the analysis of prayers left at Thierenbach[5] (Herberich-Marx 1991). All three data sources are from the 1980s, so that they all give information about contemporary manifestations of popular religiosity.

Analysis and interpretation of data

The inscriptions are in majority anonymous: about a half is unsigned or has only initials. The signed inscriptions do not reveal the identity of the authors: most contain only the first name which does not permit their identification. Women are by far the most frequent writers of messages to the Virgin: for every 100 women there are only 15.3 men. This result confirms that popular religion is to a large extent the domain of women.

The age of the writers of messages could be studied only indirectly, by studying their themes. Namely, the themes such as success at school or at University point without doubt to the age of their writers. Such indications are also contained in the prayers for love, especially of the type "may I please start dating this boy/that girl". If we assume that these messages were written by the persons in their teens and twenties, then it can be posited that at least about a half of the messages were written by a young population – mainly high school and university population.

The messages are in general short. Almost all are written in prose, without any specific stylistic characteristics. Only a few authors have presented their message in verse (either quoting a poem or making it up) or in the form of a customary prayer. Altogether, the mess-

Table 1. Requests by themes.

Theme	#	%
1	309	20.0
2	283	18.3
3	268	17.4
4	206	13.3
5	145	9.4
6	119	7.7
7	101	6.5
8	60	3.9
9	54	3.5
Total	1545	100.0

ages are not individualized: due to little variation in form, they exhibit great similarity.

The messages are in most cases requests, thanksgivings or praises (by which respect is paid to the Virgin or her glory is extolled). More than 90% of all messages are requests, either only requests or requests in combination with a thanksgiving or a praise. We also note 20% of thanksgivings either alone or in combination with a request. There are only two messages, which although they do not have a classic form of a vow, contain a request and a pledge that the person will do something in return for the Virgin's help. For example:

"Although I have sometimes been a bit evil, forgive me and give me strength to stand every temptation, and I promise you fidelity."

Next I have analyzed themes of all requests notwithstanding whether they appear alone or in combination with another type of message. In each message there are on the average one and a half themes for which a person prays the Virgin. For the purposes of analysis the themes of requests have been categorized as follows (cf. Čapo 1992):

1. requests referring to everyday activities – school, work, etc.;
2. requests referring to love, marriage, and children;
3. general requests for help and granting of prayers;
4. requests for happiness, satisfaction, peace, understanding etc.;
5. requests for guarding, protection, and the Virgin's constant presence;
6. requests for health;
7. requests for conversion, strong faith, forgiveness or deliverance from sins, also requests for strength, patience, obedience etc.;
8. requests referring to the war in Croatia 1991/1992;
9. other requests encompassing various themes, for example travelling, losing weight, going to the seaside, requests in which existential problems are mentioned as an incentive for prayer (troubles, sorrows, anxieties, sufferings, etc.), etc.

Three most frequent requests directed to the Virgin refer to school, love and general help. About the same number of requests contain these three themes. All other themes, except the one for happiness, appear in less than a tenth of all cases. Most numerous are school-related prayers of which one fifth contain a very concrete request for immediate help:

"Mother of God help me get three[6] in history today. Many thanks."

The second most frequent theme is related to love, mostly to the beginning of a love affair, to settlement of a disagreement between lovers and to the duration of love. Only rarely do these requests refer to marriage or to having children. The use of informal language (slang) is still another point in the argument that we are dealing with a relatively young population:

"Oh blessed Mother, please help me start dating L. (first name)."

In the third most frequent category we find prayers for general, unspecified help. Those requests in which the theme is unspecified because it is believed that the Virgin knows what the request is about, have been added to this group. Requests for happiness and blessing are somewhat more specific than the previous ones. Protection, either in the form "defend me" or "be near me", is searched for all day and night, and everywhere. In the rare cases in which the reason for protection is specified, it is against evil (people) and the satan, i. e. against an abstract danger.

The next most frequent category are the requests for one's own or somebody else's health. Generally, they do not mention a specific illness from which the person praying for help (or in whose behalf it is prayed) suffers. There-

Table 2. Messages according to beneficiary.

Beneficiary	#	%	Others	#	%
Just oneself	619	61.9	Parents/brothers	132	30.5
Just others	132	13.2	Family	115	26.6
Oneself+others	221	22.1	General	90	20.8
No indication	28	2.8	Partner	55	12.7
			Children	20	4.6
			Other	21	4.8
Total	1000	100.0	Total	433[8]	100.0

fore, they are probably just general expressions of concern for health by people who are not necessarily ill. The requests referring to faith, salvation, finding the right way and living like a Christian account for a relatively small number of cases.

Finally, there are prayers referring to the war in Croatia in 1991/1992, mostly prayers for its end, for peace in Croatia, and for the return of soldiers and refugees:

"Oh, blessed Virgin Mary make that I return to Baranya[7] (name)."

It is possible to study the extent to which people pray only for themselves and/or include other people in their messages. A difference was made between messages in which a person prays for himself/herself and/or for others (entire family, particular members of the family, other relatives, etc.).

About 80% of all messages contain a prayer in behalf of the person who has written it; in only 35% cases do they contain a prayer in behalf of another person. In most cases people pray for members of the family (parents, brothers and sisters), for the family as a unit (without specifying its members[9]), and generally for "us" or for "Croats", "Croatia", for "our village" and alike. The high proportion of the messages in behalf of parents (and brothers and sisters) and the low proportion of those in behalf of children corroborate the hypothesis brought out on the basis of other analyses that the population writing these messages is young.

The theme of the message is also a function of its beneficiary. The messages in one's own behalf more or less repeat the pattern of themes found in all messages (this is expected because they account for the biggest number of messages). But in the messages in behalf of others, either of the whole family or its members, the pattern of themes changes, with health, general help, protection and happiness taking over from the most frequent themes in all messages (school, love).

The entire dataset exhibits the following pattern of the appellation of the Virgin.

The Virgin is most frequently called "mother"[10], either only "mother" or "the Mother of God", "Dear Mother" or "Mother Mary". A most noticeable feature of the appellation of the Virgin is the absence of the local denomination (as e.g. "Our Lady of Osijek"). Nor is she ever called "Our Lady of Lourdes". Some people refer to the Virgin as if she were their own mother:

Table 3. Appellation of the Virgin.

Most frequent	#	Noun	#	Adjective	#
Mother of God	286	Mother	600	"Of God"	288
Dear Mother	64	Mary	120	Dear	93
Mother Mary	58	Lady	27	Saint	41
Dear Mother of God	17	Little mother	14	My/our	31
		Virgin	12	Blessed	8
				Superlative	9

"Mother thank you for bringing me to the world. My heart lives for your love for me. I return you all with love. Your son (first name)."

Regularly the Virgin is addressed with a familiar and not with a respectful form "you".[11] The concluding words of the messages also point to the familiarity and warmth with which the people address the Virgin, for example: "yours", "always yours", "loves you yours", "thankful", "loyal", "your sweet", "your angel", "your sheep", etc.

In 24 messages another saint or divine person is mentioned besides the Virgin: God, Jesus Christ, St. Leopold Mandić[12], St. Anthony, etc. People address them either directly or indirectly *via* the Virgin. In 13.6% cases it is only God to whom the message is directed. Notwithstanding the person(s) to whom the message is addressed, all messages have the same form and themes.

Comparison between prayers in Osijek and elsewhere

A marked difference between messages in Osijek and those found at Trsat (Adriatic coast) concerns the themes of the messages and, closely linked to this feature, the age of the population writing them. It can be argued that the young age of the population who leaves messages in Osijek is a function of the medium in which the messages are written – as wall inscriptions in the chapel of Our Lady of Lourdes. At the same time age has an effect on the themes of messages. In other words, it can be posited that the themes of inscriptions are directly a function of age and indirectly of the medium in which they are written. The themes testify to primary interests of younger people: good results at school and at university, and love (wishes to meet somebody, problems with partners, etc.). Two other main themes, having a somewhat smaller percentage, are more general – search for help and a request for a happier life. Besides the latter two, the majority of cases at Trsat, refer to the general requests for health and protection, neither of which specifies the illness or the danger against which help is sought. In general, the themes of requests at Trsat are not in direct relation with some concrete problem.

In contradistinction, in Osijek themes are so concrete that the examples are not rare (one fifth of all requests regarding school) in which a person mentions the exact date when the Virgin's help is needed – for example, to meet today a person whom one likes, not to get a bad mark in the test to be written tomorrow, etc. Young people seek concrete help, now and here; not in an unspecified time and place, but today or tomorrow, at school, in the street or at home.

The function of the church of St. Peter and Paul in Osijek might contribute to the concreteness and immediacy of the inscriptions. While at Trsat it could be hypothesized that the motivation of believers to come to Trsat is not a concrete need or thanksgiving but an array of various motives, and that maybe the most frequent incentive to go is that the parish to which the believer belongs organizes a pilgrimage to Trsat (Čapo 1992), a similar inference cannot be made in Osijek. The Osijek church is not a pilgrimage center such as Trsat, but a parish church in the center of Osijek; here people do not come in organized groups, but individually; and, it appears based on this analysis, not with an insufficiently defined motive. Quite on the contrary, it seems that a good number of people visit the church on deliberation, to express a specific, concrete need (i. e. a request prompts them to come to the church). This points both to the presence of the Virgin in the everyday life of people, and to the practice to call upon her when one is in trouble. There is also room for assuming that some people come without a well defined purpose, and that inspired by the walls covered up with messages, they want to leave their trace, maybe out of the same wish and need for a lasting noting down of one's name and exploits that has been attributed to the authors of glagolitic inscriptions (Fučić 1982: 18), or maybe out of a challenge brought about by the writing on a wall: risk of time pressure, secrecy of the act, limitation of the medium (cf. Thévoz 1988: 216 speaking of graffiti), possibly even transgression that the act involves.

The young people who succumb to the challenge of the wall are preoccupied with their own problems – school and love – therefore they mostly pray for themselves, and to a much lesser extent in behalf of other people. At Trsat, where, it has been proposed, people of various ages leave messages, the number of the messages in behalf of other people is double its number in Osijek. The age determines also who these other people are – parents, mother, father, sister, brother, family in general in Osijek; family in general and children at Trsat. It is argued that age differences are at the root of these differences.

There is still another specificity of these messages, which is not a function of the age nor of the medium, but of the actual social and political circumstances during which some messages were written – the war in Croatia 1991/1992. A negligible number of people who left messages at Trsat in 1987 prayed for unknown people, for the wider community in which they lived or for some other community (which at that moment was afflicted by war, hunger, etc.), or for all people in the world. Most people were self-centered and concerned only with their narrowest family and its problems. Based on these findings it has been proposed that the primary reference group of a contemporary (wo)man is in the first place (her) his family. It has been posited that all (her) his interests, wishes and needs are exhausted within that small social group (Čapo 1992). During the period 1991/1992 in which some inscriptions were written the sociopolitical circumstances were drastically changed, and one could not, in spite of one's own preoccupations (and youth which is turned onto itself) be indifferent towards wider community – one's village, town, region, entire Croatia and its inhabitants. The war took on such proportions and brought about such consequences that everybody was affected by it in a direct or indirect way.

Another difference is that the inscriptions in which a person does not address the Virgin but God or another saint are more frequent in Osijek than in Trsat. This is another evidence of the character of these sanctuaries: Trsat is a renowned pilgrimage center with a miraculous Virgin, and Osijek is a parish church dedicated to St. Peter and Paul in which a person need not address specifically the Mother of God. There seems to be no difference in the addressing of either the Virgin or God: expressions, themes, and forms of familiarity are the same. There is no ground for asserting that God is less attainable and less accessible than the Virgin, or that the believer more willingly and more easily communicates with his intercessor – the Virgin.

The Virgin is called only "mother", or "the Mother of God", and not "the Mother of God of Lourdes" or "of Osijek". She does not have the local denomination because the statue represents the apparition of the Virgin to the little Bernardette at Lourdes, i. e. it has no relation to Osijek, and because, no miraculous event has been linked to the statue since its placing in Osijek at the beginning of this century. The fact that the Virgin is never called "Our Lady of Lourdes" can be explained either as ignorance or failure of the authors of the messages to recognize the iconography of the statue or even, as a successful education of believers in the period after the Council of Vatican in which, in contradistinction to the popular view that saints might have variant forms, the uniqueness of the Virgin has been reasserted (cf. Čapo 1991).

The mentioned differences notwithstanding, the messages to the Virgin at Trsat and in Osijek do exhibit some similarities. At both places the relative share of gender among the authors is more or less the same: women, regardless of age, address the Virgin in a far bigger number than men. The Virgin seems to take a prominent place in the life of people visiting these two places. She is their helper, protector, donator, leader, forgiving mother redeemer and savior. People of different ages do not only confide in her, but expect that she will make decisions instead of them and help them resolve difficult situations. Furthermore, sure that the Virgin will gratify their requests, they thank her in advance. Both in Osijek and at Trsat the cases in which a request contains a pledge of some act in exchange for the gratification of the request (a vow) are exceptional.

Finally, the comparison of messages from

two Croatian sanctuaries and from a French one can be summarized as follows. There is a marked difference between the Croatian and French messages in addressing the Virgin: first, in the appellation – "the Mother of God" vs. "Notre-Dame" ("Our Lady") and "Vierge Miraculeuse" ("Miraculous Virgin"), and second, in the form of addressing (familiar versus respectful "you" form). In all other respects (e. g. themes, beneficiaries, etc.), the messages from Trsat and Thierenbach are more similar than the messages from Osijek and Trsat. The messages at Trsat and Thierenbach exhibit similarities in the form and content of the communication with the divine, in which ethnic and cultural differences between the two countries seem to be overriden by the common features of Roman-Catholic popular religiosity. These features are also present in the form of the Osijek messages, as well as in the idea that a person can pray the Virgin for help, but in most other respects the messages found in Osijek are different. This is attributed above all to the difference in the age structure of the authors of the messages at respective places and to the function of the churches. It is likely that the authors of the messages at both Trsat and Thierenbach are distributed more or less evenly across all age groups.[13] The younger people, who introduce into their messages other interests than the middle aged or older people, predominate in Osijek mostly because the messages are written on the wall, in a medium that, one assumes, is considered inappropriate by the people of middle and older ages. The differences might also result from the function of the church – the sanctuaries at Trsat and Thierenbach are well-known pilgrimage centers dedicated to the Virgin, while the Osijek church is a local church dedicated to St. Peter and Paul and with no pilgrimage tradition in the usual sense. It is only known as such by a certain age group of the inhabitants of Osijek. That makes it such a unique dataset for research.[14]

Notes

1. Glagolitic alphabet is an old Croatian alphabet, used until the 19th century in the coastal Croatia, but also in some parts of continental Croatia, mainly in liturgy and in pious publications.
2. Their contents vary covering a wide range from prayers to comments of social events, notices on epidemics that struck a region, etc.
3. These inscriptions have possibly one more of the features of graffiti. According to Grasskamp (1988: 199) they are magic which manifests itself at the very moment of the writing. To the magic contained in the moment of writing one can add the magic of the inscriptions themselves, if we take them to be a kind of a magical invocation.
4. Trsat is a well known Croatian pilgrimage centre located on the northern Adriatic coast. I have presented the results of the analysis of those prayers at the 11th Mariological Congress held in Huelva, Spain in September 1992 (Čapo 1992).
5. Thierenbach is found in Alsace, France.
6. The grading system ranges from 1 (insufficient) to 5 (excellent).
7. Baranya is the easternmost region of Croatia (between the rivers Danube and Drava). At the moment it is under the Serbian occupation and its Croatian population has been expelled.
8. This number does not correspond to the number of prayers for other people (see the same table), because a message can contain prayers in behalf of more than one person.
9. The messages for the family as a unit and for individual family members have been separately categorized because they seem to be a function of the age of the population who writes them: middle aged and older people make requests in behalf of the family as a unit, and younger ones in behalf of particular family members.
10. Usually written with a capital letter, but frequently the whole message is capitalized.
11. For the second personal pronoun in Singular, Croatian distinguishes between a familiar you form (*du* or *tu* in German and French respectively) and a respectful you form (*Sie* or *Vous* in German and French).
12. The only Croatian saint.
13. To some extent this statement runs contrary to the conclusion of Mme. Herberich-Marx regarding the age of the people visiting Thierenbach.
14. A broader version of this paper will be published in Croatian in the journal *Studia ethnologica croatica* V, 1993.

References

Billeter, Fritz 1988: Harald Naegeli izaziva pažnju svojim nacrtanim likovima (Harald Naegeli draws attention with his drawn figures), In: *Quorum* 1(18): 223–224 (original in German).
Clifford, James 1986: Introduction: Partial Truths.

In: J. Clifford & G. E. Marcus (eds.): *Writing Culture. The Poetics and Politics of Ethnography*, Berkeley: University of California Press, pp. 1–26.

Čapo, Jasna 1991: Sveti likovi, svete vodice i zavjeti. O hodočašćima hrvatskoga življa u madarskoj Baranji (Holy Images, Holy Waters and Vows. Pilgrimages of Croatians in Hungarian Baranya), In: *Etnološka tribina* 14: 17–50.

Čapo, Jasna 1992: *Etnološka obradba suvremenih proštenjarskih zapisa na Trsatu* (Ethnological Analysis of Contemporary Pilgrims' Messages at Trsat), Paper presented at the XI Mariological Congress at Huelva, Spain.

Fainzang, Sylvie 1991: Suppliques à Notre-Dame de Bonne Garde. Construire l'efficacité des prières de guérison, In: *Archives de sciences sociales des Religions* 73: 63–79.

Fučić, Branko 1982: *Glagoljaški natpisi* (Glagolitic inscriptions), Zagreb: JAZU.

Gamboni, Dario 1988: Skice odlaska i povratka: grafiti, vandalizam, cenzura i razaranje (Sketches of Leaving and Coming back: Graffiti, Vandalism, Censorship and Destruction), In: *Quorum* 1(18): 213–214 (original in German).

Grasskamp, Walter 1988: Rukopis izdaje (Handwriting deceives), In: *Quorum* 1(18): 197–204 (original in German).

Herberich-Marx, Geneviève 1991: *Evolution d'une sensibilité religieuse. Témoignages scripturaires et iconographiques de pèlerinages alsaciens*. Strasbourg: Presses universitaires de Strasbourg.

Horvat, Andela 1956: *Spomenici arhitekture i likovnih umjetnosti u Medumurju* (Monuments of Architecture and Pictural Art in Medumurje), Zagreb.

Horvat, Andela 1975: *Izmedu gotike i baroka, Umjetnost kontinentalnog dijela Hrvatske od oko 1500. do oko 1700.* (Between Gothic and Baroque. The art of Continental Croatia between around 1500 and 1700), Zagreb: Društvo povjesničara umjetnosti Hrvatske.

Lalić, Dražen 1991: Pojam grafita (The Notion of Graffiti), In: D. Lalić, A. Leburić & N. Bulat: *Grafiti i subkultura* (Graffiti and Subculture), Zagreb: Alinea, pp. 29–36.

Skasa-Weiss, Ruprecht 1988: Grafiti – zidno slikarstvo ili vandalizam? (Graffiti – Wall Art or Vandalism?), In: *Quorum* 1(18): 205–212 (original in German).

Thévoz, Michel 1988: Zid kao erogena zona (Wall as Erogenic Zone), In: *Quorum* 1(18): 215–217 (original in German).

Velčić, Mirna 1991: *Otisak priče. Intertekstualno proučavanje autobiografije* (Traces of Stories. Intertextual Study of Autobiographies), Zagreb: August Cesarec.

Popular Cosmology on the Threshold of the 20th Century

Ulrika Wolf-Knuts

Wolf-Knuts, Ulrika 1994: Popular Cosmology on the Threshold of the 20th Century. Ethnologia Europaea 24: 77–81.

The basis of my study is formed by a written material which was gathered in 1903 amongst Swedish-speaking Finns. Seven subject areas are covered: religion, mother tongue, geography, general history, arithmetic, geometry, and knowledge of nature. Several questions are answered according to an understanding of the world which is based on three aspects: the different subjects' own experience of physical existence, the teaching of the Church, and in some cases, on the reading of books. The worldview contained in those folklore narratives which also have cosmological themes is of a different nature. The analysis attempts to demonstrate how different worldviews are described in an interview and in narratives, respectively. *Bricolage* and codeswitching are scientific concepts used for this purpose.

Ulrika Wolf-Knuts, Dr., Reader, Department of History of Religion and Folkloristics, Åbo Akademi University, SF-20500 Turku, Finland.

It is a well known fact that the word "worldview" has different meanings (cf. Knuuttila 1989:171). Concepts like "overall covering", "value system", "fundamental attitude" show that students with a philosophically sophisticated orientation think of worldview as something coherent, a consistent whole (Pentikäinen 1980: 238, Kurtén 1991: 1). But is it equally homogeneous and consistent among people who lack a philosophical and theological education? According to Knuuttila it is, however, impossible to consider the folk worldview inferior as regards its intellectual substance, since it can only partly be explained by the scientific one (Knuuttila 1989: 206).

Research on worldview can be divided into four different periods. First students concentrated upon the view of the physical environment, i.e. of cosmology. Thereafter they devoted themselves to the cultural meaning of this cosmology and as a corollary paid attention to the fundamental ideas of the worldviews. Now students claim that worldview is a logical whole consisting of disparate parts, and that it is necessary to look for the elements which constitute this logical whole.

To me worldview means cosmology, i.e. the idea of the universe, its genesis, evolution, and structure (cf. Dundes 1978: 118). I intend to examine a specific material in which six different persons from the same milieu describe their worldviews. Is this folk worldview logical and consistent? I assume that the cosmology as a common cultural heritage is fairly constant and that it should consequently generate fairly uniform descriptions.

My material was collected in 1903 by Hugo R. Sjöberg (1867–1941) at Replot, a Swedish-speaking fishing community in the Vasa archipelago, Finland. It consists of 210 questions and answers concerning six different disciplines, i.e. religion, geography, common history, mathematics, geometry and science. The answers were given by three women and three men aged 20–30 years, 40–50 years and 70–80 years. The informants were not able to write very well. This material is supplemented by some folkloristic records by Sjöberg (Sjöberg 1984: 11f). The informants never refer to each other, so probably Sjöberg interviewed them independently.

The creation of the world is given religious

and scientific explanations combined with *praxis* (Asplund 1991:10). The myths of the Bible make up the starting point for the ideas of how the world was made, but especially concerning the Replot archipelago, i.e. the environment of the informants, the picture of God is completed by a giant as creator.

The world can be divided into several parts. Heaven is above man, one informant was even skeptical as to whether heaven exists at all. Earth is said to lie on an axis, a needle or a point, which guarantees that it remains in space. But it can also rest on almighty God. Space is inhabited by living beings, i.e. the spirits of the dead. In folklore these spirits can walk around on earth and appear before living people (Sjöberg 1984: 72f, 75, 77ff). The moon is described in scientific terms, there is no idea of a man in the moon (cf. af Klintberg 1988: 203ff).

The interior of the earth can be compact with mud, sand, stones and water which serve as nourishment for the plants, but the poisons of the earth are what frogs feed on. In the earth live some animals and also people; one informant even talked about a sunken city somewhere in America. In folklore there is a tradition of underground beings who can steal people's children. Hell is said to be in the underworld, in the sea, on earth or high up across the heavens. What is behind the sun and the stars is either unknown, or said to be more land and earth, or is explained by something God has created. When explaining the structure of the cosmos, the informants combine scientific knowledge, like astronomy, physics and biology, with facts from religion, folklore, *praxis* and common history.

The informants claim that the world is as round as a ball, because on the open sea they have got their personal experience of the horizon as a circle. The earth is kept in balance thanks to the axis or to God's omnipotence, but on the other hand it is said to go round, too. The power that keeps all things and human beings on earth is said to be the air, gravity or God's power. Science, like geometry and astronomy, is combined with religion, folklore and *praxis*.

The world changes. Some natural phenomena, like rivers and mountains, grow. Earthquakes and erosion explain changes, and the uplift of the land, which is very remarkable at Replot, is a real experience of changes in the landscape. But the earth has also changed as it has become more sinful.

Eternity lasts forever but is incomprehensible. But it is also seen as a synonym for hell, due to a cited verse: "O eternity, your length frightens me", or to the idea of eternity as being worse than life, because it is said, probably in some devotional book, that the worldly punishment is nothing compared with the eternal one. A more mathematical explanation tells us that eternity has neither a beginning nor an end. Here, too, *praxis*, science, folklore, religion and history are combined.

Cosmology is thus described within several disciplines. The informants use concepts from the Bible and the Lutheran church, folklore and experience. The ideas are used indiscriminately, sometimes complementing each other, sometimes contradictory. On this level the folk cosmology does not seem to be logical or consistent. It is nothing new, though, that folk ways of thinking are not consistent. Folk ideas can even be diametrical (Dundes 113ff). Lévi-Strauss introduces the concept of *bricolage* in order to explain the folk way, or rather, the mythical way of thinking as opposed to scientific thinking. *Bricolage* means that man uses only limited resources for his thinking, he never adds new elements, but he is able to construct new constellations of the existing components, constellations which he can use when necessary (1968: 29ff).

I would like to see the cosmological knowledge of the Replot inhabitants as a *bricolage*. How is it composed? The answers to the religious questions contain religious, historical and practical elements. The answers to the geographical questions contain religious, scientific, practical and geometrical elements. The answers to the historical questions contain folklore, religious, scientific and practical elements. The scientific questions are answered by religious, scientific, practical, and folklore elements. The conditions for a *bricolage* are fulfilled. The common theme is cosmology, the elements of thought are found in the knowledge that the informants have from the different disciplines, folklore and *praxis*, and at the same time these elements are also limited by the disciplines, folklore and *praxis*. These elements are used in situations created by the interviewer. By combining the elements in different ways the informants can explain cosmology as required.

Thus, cosmology can be described in many different ways with concepts from many different spheres of knowledge. Still, it is the same world that is described, but different dimensions are pointed out in different situations and different contexts. The descriptions of cosmology depend on the narrator's, i.e. the ego's needs to understand and shape. By different forms of socialization (school, church, practical life, tradition) man has a store of ingredients (thoughts and conceptions of heaven, earth, the underworld and so forth), from which, under propitious circumstances (incentives from outside) he can collect elements for a cosmology to fit in a certain situation. In another situation he can fetch other useful elements. What keeps the elements/ingredients together is the sum made up of his knowledge and the situational needs, i.e. the situational context, which also decides what dimension should be accentuated.

This observation is combined with McConvell's model for codeswitching, a word used to describe a situation typical of multilingual communities, i.e. "the use of more than one language in the course of a single communicative episode" (Heller 1988: 1). McConvell shows how a speaker, in his communication with a partner, uses a certain strategy which is founded on the relations between the speaker himself, the addressee and the topic. These relations are, in fact, central in the speaking situation. According to McConvell not only the addressee's ability to understand the message is essential, as communication studies often put it (cf. Bringéus 1979: 9ff); the theme or the referent is also of the utmost significance because it represents the speaker's position in the social arena in relation to the addressee. The referent decides what code of language should be used, and the speaker can in certain situations emphasize particular relations between himself, the addressee, and the referent, whereas he simultaneously de-emphasizes other relations (McConvell 1988: 102ff, 111). Codeswitching is illustrated by concentric circles, nested layers, which in McConvell's examples represent different language speaker-sets consisting of a local dialect, a normal language for a linguistic minority and the official language of the local majority (ibid.107). McConvell describes "a specific type of situation where otherwise mutually exclusive social arenas can be called into play during the course of a single social interaction" (Heller 1988: 17).

The term codeswitching is, however, limited to the change of language, but in my material there is no shift between different languages. This particular term cannot therefore be used here, but it is inspiring for my further considerations. In my material the informants change their means of expression on a semantic level rather than on a linguistic one. The world can be explained in several different ways although the same language is used. The informants choose different means of expression by picking resources from different spheres of knowledge or different cultural contexts. Thus, the way of describing, i.e. the mode, changes and therefore codeswitching could be replaced by modeswitching.

Just as the different languages in codeswitching can be related to each other as nested layers, so it is possible to look upon the different spheres of knowledge in modeswitching as concentric circles. It is, however, easier to define a switch between two different languages than between two different cultural spheres. The borderline between these, and at the same time between the concentric circles, cannot in fact be definite and fixed, and all circles are kept together by something, namely the theme, the referent. It is therefore more appropriate to think of a kaleidoscope which already contains all the ingredients but which also allows reorganisation when needed. A kaleidoscope contains all the parts needed in order to create a new constellation, a new image of reality. Man's thought can thus be said to be kaleidoscopic and can be changed according to the situation within the frames of a given theme, the referent, by means of given elements of thought. The limits between religion, science, geography, history, folklore, and *praxis* are vague in describing cosmologies. Elements from the different spheres are mixed into a *bricolage*. According to this it would be more efficient to introduce the term modemixing instead of modeswitching.

The descriptions of the cosmology can be seen in a kaleidoscopic perspective. In my case the theme cosmology constitutes the frames of the kaleidoscope. When the interviewer Sjöberg brings cosmology to the fore in a religious context, the speaker is able to turn his "intellectual" kaleidoscope so that the terminology prevalent in religious descriptions proves useful. In a corresponding way he can use the kaleidoscope within the other spheres of knowledge, too. The relation between speaker and referent is thus central, as was the case in codeswitching. The informants can also answer questions from one sphere by modemixing between several spheres. Folklore, however, seems to be an exception, because in the texts collected within the frames of a folkloristic recording, cosmology is described only by folkloristic concepts. But folkloristic elements of thought were rather often used within other spheres of thought.

In all spheres except folklore God is introduced as a component in thinking. So he is a frequently repeated element in the kaleidoscope and it is possible for man to use him in varying connections. This happens especially when the informants' knowledge in other spheres does not suffice. They seem to think of God in cosmology when something is impossible to explain by other means.

Thus, thinking of cosmology is constructed by knowledge and experience, and where these factors do not suffice, the informants attribute it to the omnipotent God (Spilka et al. 1985). So the otherwise disparate set of different descriptions of cosmology has a logical consistency – provided that "logical" does not mean "scientifically logical", but appropriate and practical in the informant's present situation, like a *bricolage*. By attribution the informants use a functional logic as they show a complementary way of thinking. My material thus shows that the inhabitants of Replot command many types of cosmologies, which do not necessarily have to be consistent, but it shows also that the informants know how to create consistency.

The fact that in folklore God holds an exceptional position, which means that he is not mentioned as an explanation in the cosmology of folklore, can be due to the way the recordings were made. The collectors' view of folklore as something other than normal culture may be the reason why, in folkloristic connections, the informants avoided referring to scientific or practical knowledge. In the same way it is possible that their methods of posing questions has steered the informants forwards to a special folkloristic sphere, where they did not associate with other forms of culture. This must be taken into consideration today in analysing the folk worldview.

References

Helsingfors / Helsinki
Svenska Litteratursällskapet i Finland/The Society of Swedish Literature in Finland
Folkkultursarkivet/Folklore Archive
SLS 86: Folktron vid tjugonde seklets början. Sammanställd i frågor och svar af H.R.A. Sjöberg.

Asplund, Johan. 1991. *Essä om Gemeinschaft och Gesellschaft*. Göteborg: Bokförlaget Korpen.
Bringéus, Nils-Arvid. 1979. Kommunikationsaspekten inom etnologi och folkloristik. In *Kulturell kommunikation*, ed. Nils-Arvid Bringéus & Göran Rosander, pp. 9–21. Lund: Signum.
Dundes, Alan. 1978. *Essays in Folkloristics*. Meerut: Folklore Institute.
Heller, Monica. 1988. Introduction. In *Codeswitching*, ed. Monica Heller, pp. 1–24. Berlin: Mouton de Gruyter.
af Klintberg, Bengt. 1988. Myter om månens fläckar. In *Tal över blandade ämnen*, pp. 203–222. Uppsala: Collegium curiosorum novum. Årsbok 1985/86.
Knuuttila, Seppo. 1989. Kansanomainen maailmankuva. In Manninen, Juha & al., *Maailmankuva kulttuurin kokonaisuudessa*, pp. 165–223. Oulu: Pohjoinen.
Kurtén, Tage. 1991. *Livsåskådningar och intervjuer – begreppsliga och metodiska problem*. Åbo. (Stencil).
Lévi-Strauss, Claude. 1968. *Das wilde Denken*. Frankfurt am Main: Suhrkamp.
McConvell, Patrick. 1988. Mix-im-up: aboriginal code-switching, old and new. In *Codeswitching*,

ed. Monica Heller, pp. 97–149. Berlin: Mouton de Gruyter.
Pentikäinen, Juha. 1980. Yksilö perinteentutkimuksen kohteena. In *Perinteentutkimuksen perusteita*, ed. Outi Lehtipuro, pp. 185–248. Porvoo: WSOY.
Sjöberg, H.R.A. 1984. *Livet bland Kvarkens söner och döttrar* 1–2. Vasa: Replot Ungdomsförenings museikommitté.
Spilka, Bernard et al. 1985. A general attribution theory for the psychology of religion. *Journal for the scientific study of religion* 24: 1–20.

Current Activities

Swedish Modernity and Everyday Life
An International Course at Lund University

From January through June 1995 the Department of European Ethnology and the Department of Sociology at Lund University offers for the second time a course on the cultural analysis of everyday life: *Swedish Modernity and Everyday Life: Cultural and Social Perspectives*. This course develops innovative theoretical and methodological approaches to the study of modern society and culture. The analytic tools taught are applicable to any complex culture and society, but the empirical basis of the course is the development of everyday life and social institutions in 20th century Sweden. The Swedish experience is used for a comparative discussion of the ways in which different modern societies have developed and how classes, gender, age-groups, regions, and nations are constructed culturally and socially within this framework. Thus, this course not only aims to facilitate students' understanding of Swedish culture, but also to present new approaches to the social and cultural analysis of modern life in general.

We kindly ask you to make interested students and colleagues aware of this course which is aimed at students who already have some background in the field of social or cultural studies (such as ethnology, folklore, sociology, anthropology, cultural studies, social history, etc.), or who have taken one of the introductory courses on Swedish society offered by the University of Lund. This means that we expect students to be either well under way with their undergraduate studies or in the beginning of their graduate studies. All readings and lectures will be in English. Thus, to be able to participate in the course it is required that students be able to express themselves in both written and spoken English. The course workload will be the equivalent of one term's full-time university study.

The course will be taught primarily in seminar form. Students will be expected and encouraged to contribute actively in discussions. The course will also involve some fieldwork and projects both as individual and as group work. There will also be excursions and visits to different urban and rural Swedish settings. *There are no tuition fees for this course*.

The last application date is *September the 15th, 1994*. If enrolment is not full after this date, we will consider applications up until the start of the course.

For application form and further information write:

Department of European Ethnology
Student advisor
Finngatan 8
S – 223 62 Lund
Sweden
Tel. + 46 46 10 75 66
Fax + 46 46 10 42 05

The Gypsy Lore Society
17th Annual Conference 1995

The Gypsy Lore Society will hold its Annual Meeting and Conference on Gypsy Studies at the State University of Leiden, Leiden, Netherlands. The meeting, the 17th in the series of annual conferences begun by the Gypsy Lore Society, North American Chapter, will take place May 29–31, 1995. Papers on any aspect of Gypsy, Traveller or related peripatetic studies are welcome. Abstracts of 125 words must be received by November 15, 1994. Please send abstracts and enquiries to Aparna Rao, Program Coordinator, Institut für Völkerkunde, Universität zu Köln, Albertus-Magnus-Platz, D-50923 Köln, Germany.

Tel. + 49 221 470 2278/4088
Fax + 49 221 470 5117
Internet: alv04@rsl.rrz.uni-koeln.de

Instructions to authors

Manuscripts should be sent to the editorial address mentioned below. They may be forwarded to members of the editoral board for evaluation, but the final decision rests with the editor. Authors will be notified as quickly as possible about acceptance, rejection, or desired alterations.

Papers should generally *not exceed 30 printed pages* (of 4500 type units). Illustrations with captions should be sent together with the text. The author will receive the first proof – which is a page proof – while the second is only read by the editor. Alterations against the manuscripts will normally not be accepted.

The author will get a free supply of 30 *offprints*. Additional copies must be ordered in connection with the return of the proof.

Manuscripts in *English* will be preferred. Manuscripts in German or French should be supplied with a *summary* in English.

An abstract in the language of the paper should accompany the manuscript. It should be short (100–125 words), outline the main features and stress the conclusions.

Typescript: Page 1 should contain (1) title, (2) name(s) of author(s) (3) abstract, and (4) author's full postal address (including title, name and institution). The text should start on page 2.

The use of italics is indicated by underlining. Desired position of illustrations should be marked with pencil in left margin. Too many grades of headings should be avoided.

Long quotations should not be marked by indentations, but only indicated by quotation marks and double line spacing before and after.

Notes and references: Notes should be reserved for additional information or comments. Bibliographic references in the text are given as: Gurevich (1981: 17) or (Hobsbawm & Ranger 1983).

In the list of references the following usage is adopted:

For journals or composite works:

Christiansen, Palle O. 1979: Peasant Adaptation to Bourgeois Culture? In: *Ethnologia Scandinavica:* 98–151.

Hofer, Tamás: Phasen des Wandels im östlichen Mitteleuropa. In: G. Wiegelmann (ed.): *Kultureller Wandel im 19. Jht.* Göttingen: 251–264.

For books:

Burke, Peter 1978: *Popular Culture in Early Modern Europe.* London.

Hall, Stuart, & Tony Jefferson (eds.) 1976: *Resistance through Rituals.* London.

Editorial address:
Professor Bjarne Stoklund
Institute of Archaeology and Ethnology
Vandkunsten 5
DK-1467 Copenhagen
Denmark

Ethnologia Europaea
Journal of European Ethnology

Contents of volume 24:1

Editorial: Ethnization of Culture	3
Konrad Köstlin: Das ethnographische Paradigma	5
Peter Niedermüller: Politics, Culture and Social Symbolism	21
Bjarne Stoklund: The Role of the International Exhibitions	35
Gizela Welz: Putting a Mirror to People's Lives	45
Žita Škovierová: Ethnic Consciousness and Cohabitation	51
Balasz Balogh: Ungarndeutsche in Geretsried	59
Jasna Čapo Žmegač: "Mother help me get a good mark in history"	67
Ulrika Wolf-Knuts: Popular Cosmology	77
Current Activities	83

ISBN 8772893052